"Illyanna brings her brilliant, sincere perspective t[o]
the impact and influence of the food of the Puerto
Boriquen people have been dispersed over generations, by every
from colonialism to Hurricane María, and Illyanna's own story is
defined by the same resilience and sazón that flavors the food of the
Isla del Encanto. *Diasporican* is a delicious journey through purpose,
place, and the power of food that you won't want to miss."
   —JOSÉ ANDRÉS, chef, cookbook author, and founder of World Central Kitchen

"Somehow, Illyanna can make you laugh out loud while you're reading
the pantry section of her cookbook. That's how bold, bright, and alive
her voice is, and that's why she has created something with *Diasporican*
that no one else could: a brilliant and heart-breaking ode to the
disconnect of diaspora identity and all the delicious fruits of such a
rupture. She ignores no pain yet lets no joke go untold as she gives us
her singular spin on a cuisine that contains seemingly endless mystery,
possibility, and flavor."
   —ALICIA KENNEDY, food writer

"This book BRINGS IT: In voice, instructions, visuals, history, education,
and hilarity—a decolonization of the cookbook world like few others."
   —GUSTAVO ARELLANO, author of *Taco USA: How Mexican Food
      Conquered America*

"Puerto Rico has a unique niche in the cuisine of the Americas, and I
can't imagine a happier situation than having Illyanna Maisonet as a
guide. *Diasporican* is the kind of book that makes you want to run to
the kitchen and then book a flight."
   —STEVE SANDO, founder and owner of Rancho Gordo

"Finally, a most overdue book that builds a bridge to understanding
and opens a door into the food and culture of Puerto Ricans. And it has
arrived from none other than Illyanna Maisonet, who has the power
to bring us all in through her raw honesty, true grit, unbridled passion,
and irresistible sazón. This is a treasure of a book—an honor to hold,
a delight to read, and a feast to cook from."
   —PATI JINICH, Mexican chef, cookbook author, and television host

Diasporican

DIASPORICAN
A Puerto Rican Cookbook

Illyanna Maisonet

Foreword by Michael W. Twitty
Puerto Rico photographs by Erika P. Rodriguez
California and food photographs by Dan Liberti

TEN SPEED PRESS
California | New York

To Margarita Galindez Maisonet (Nana)

and Carmen Nereida Maisonet (Mami)

Contents

Foreword

by Michael W. Twitty

She had me at asapao and funche, guineos turned into macabeos, steaming bowls of sancocho, and juicy pernil. The point of a good cookbook is to make you curious, fascinated, and to want to start cooking immediately. Tito Puente and Willie Colon are already in the queue and maybe some menudo. My hands are ready to get covered in garlic and achiote, I'm ready to smash some guineos, and my culo is ready to shake to keep the impatience to chow down on arroz con pollo at bay. *Diasporican* is a warm, conversational, wise work that is rooted in the values, memories, and family history that Illyanna Maisonet beautifully and matter-of-factly brings to the kitchen table. This game-changer is an invitation to the diversity and singularity of the Puerto Rican experience as a global culture.

The cookbook you are holding is a forceful love letter to a culinary tradition often sidelined and caught up in its perceived ambiguity. Puerto Rico is part of the United States—and yet it is not. It is part of Latin America but also in the sphere of North America. It is brown, it is Black, it is Caribbean, it is Iberian, it is African, and it is Native. Turn it any way you like, Puerto Rico is Puerto Rico, and the island and its people, proud and landed or ever on the move, have loyalty and love with a signature devotion for Borinquen.

Puerto Rican cuisine. Indigenous traditions of the Taino have survived, forming the backbone of Puerto Rican food and identity. Puerto Rico was one of the oldest Caribbean outposts of the Spanish empire, and with it came ingredients and ideas about food that fermented in Spain over a millennium as Iberian, North and West African, Sephardic Jewish, and Arab influences blended over the centuries. Puerto Rico also remains one of the key pinpoints in the African Atlantic. West and Central African people—Wolof, Igbo, Yoruba, Kongo, Mbundu, and many others—accomplished what they did in other parts of the African Diaspora: under the lash and labor in the sugarcane fields, they pieced together elements common to their

Arroz con jueyes, El Buren de Lula, Loíza, Puerto Rico.

Pork skin, Lechonera de Apa, Guaynabo, Puerto Rico.

Corn ice cream, King's Cream, Ponce, Puerto Rico.

civilizations and connected adjacent Native traditions to give the Puerto Rican table its soul. All these cultural pieces gave the Puerto Rican cook the ability to translate and absorb, creating an even broader edible vocabulary that moved well from Spanish Harlem to Oahu, Hawai'i, and from Hialeah, Florida, to Oakland, California.

The strength of *Diasporican* is that it moves the conversation beyond the island, drawing us into the essence of Puerto Rican food as it morphs across North America. In these pages, we go to New York, New Jersey, Connecticut, Hawai'i, Chicago, California, and beyond, getting a real sense of what matters most in Puerto Rican culture and civilization—family, friends, spirit, ancestors, rhythm, and joy-inducing flavor.

Diasporican is informed, intellectually rich, beautiful, earthy, and irreverent just like its author, my friend.

Get cooking. Ahora!

Old San Juan, Puerto Rico.

PUERTO RICO   PUERTO RICO

Mami, Burge Road Cherry Farm, Stockton, California.

Flying kites. El Catillo San Felipe del Morro, Old San Juan, Puerto Rico.

Introduction

How I became a cook is not a romantic story. I learned how to cook Puerto Rican food from my grandmother, Margarita Galindez Maisonet. Margarita was born in 1938 in the campo of Manatí, on the northern coast of the island not too far from Hacienda La Esperanza, a former sugarcane plantation. When Margarita was nine years old and in the third grade, she was sent to live with her Titi Emilia. That was the end of Margarita's formal education. That was also the end of seeing her biological mother for several decades. Margarita went to work as a "domestic" during a time when people didn't have to apologize for deep-frying their foods, when it was a way of life. There would be no passing down of heirloom cookbooks (I don't think my grandma ever owned a cookbook), words of encouragement, or time to enjoy a childhood. By the time that Margarita was fourteen years old, she was already pregnant with the first of her seven children, Carmen, my mother. Margarita, Carmen, and I became cooks out of economic necessity. We did not have the privilege of cooking for pleasure or joy. Our story is one of generational poverty and trauma with glimpses of pride and laughter, all of which have been the catalysts of ample good food in my life.

My own days begin with only the sound of my feet shuffling through dawn's sleepy light. I turn on the stove. Shuffle to the sink; the faucet knob squeaks and the aerator spits. My black pinky toenail and I wait impatiently for the spouted Le Creuset pot to fill with water. Shuffle to put the pot on the burner. The pour-over cone goes on top of the coffee mug, the coffee filter into the pour-over cone, then the coffee grounds. In the meantime, I open all the windows in the front of the house to let the morning coolness seep through the mesh screens. By the time my shuffling feet make it back to the stove, the water is bubbling. I pour the water over the coffee grounds, and the conjured smell of foggy mountains in the interior of Puerto Rico fills my California kitchen. The water sinks into and penetrates the cone, sending the dominion brew into the cup below. A flourish of cream ends my ceremony. This entire process mirrors my late grandmother's morning routine, although her pot of choice was a small aluminum Farberware made in the Bronx, and her pour-over cone was a colador. She began every waking morning with this routine, a necessary moment of meditation and coffee to galvanize her weary body into the next step—starting the daily meals, which always consisted of rice and beans.

Many of the old Puerto Rican recipes aren't quick and easy, which might be one of the reasons that the food of the island hasn't exactly taken off in the land that sits mere hours away. Another reason is probably because people don't understand the cuisine. Hell, most people don't understand us! "How can brothers and sisters from the same two parents range in color from white to Black?" they ask. Colonialism. There are white Puerto Ricans getting radical and surfing in Rincón with sun-bleached blond hair, and Black Puerto Ricans with afros creating arts and crafts in Loíza. And everything in between. And our food reflects that diversity. We know how much people love to have things simplified so it all fits neatly into a little box. The truth is, Puerto Rican cuisine shares a lot in common with the cuisines of Hawai'i, Guam, and the Philippines—all the places that got fucked by Spanish and United States colonialism. To most, Puerto Rico is just a pit stop on their boat cruise to the Bahamas. "I loved Old San Juan and mofongo" is the common response I hear when I tell someone I'm Puerto Rican. To Puerto Ricans, Puerto Rico represents a constant battle for land and a broad understanding of our identity.

When my family first came to the States and my mother was enrolled in elementary school, she didn't speak any English. During the country's Cold War–era security push, it became necessary to read and write English well, which meant that racist policies, such as the "No Spanish" rule, lingered in the newly desegregated schools. And so, my mother just didn't speak. It was a decision that would mold her personality to this day (and the reason that I don't speak Spanish). A more confrontational person might have rebelled and fought. That's not my mother's way. How could she have been confrontational at five years old? Well, ask my mom what happened when my kindergarten teacher wouldn't let me wash my hands after I went to the bathroom. All hell broke loose! I suppose because of my mother's inability to speak out, she made sure that I was the opposite of her in that way.

Anyway, during Margarita's (my nana's) first years in the States, she spent her mornings in the fields picking produce, spent her evenings in the kitchen cooking for her husband and children, and spent her nights procreating more

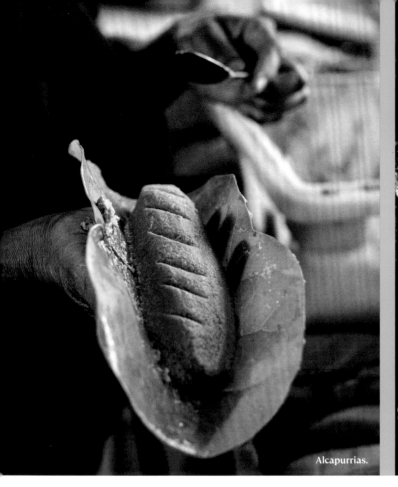

Alcapurrias.

Longaniza, El Rancho de Don Nando, Naranjito, Puerto Rico.

children. Every day. Routines and rotations of Puerto Rican recipes passed down to her from her aunt, who raised her, and her biological mother. "The mama who gave birth to me, or the mama who raised me?" she'd always clarify when asked about her mother. By the time that I arrived on this spinning marble of malachite and lapis lazuli, Nana already had a few recipes in the rotation that had been absorbed, digested, and regurgitated as "American"—spaghetti, oven barbecue, hamburgers, meatloaf, and pancakes the size of dinner plates. But she mostly made Puerto Rican food. And, for Nana, as someone who was a part of what would eventually become the 5.5 million Puerto Ricans living Stateside, mostly on the East Coast and in Florida, being on the West Coast always emphasized a pivotal issue: No one seems to know anything about Puerto Rican food. Sometimes, not even Puerto Ricans.

Puerto Ricans are quick to argue about the roots and regulations of what Puerto Rican food is. Honestly, they just love to argue. (Guilty.) There are Puerto Ricans who don't know shit about their own cuisine. No shade. That tends to happen when you believe it's your birthright; you take it for granted. Sometimes it feels like, somewhere along the line, Puerto Ricans lost their way. And with it, their food. With colonization, that isn't entirely unintentional. There can be several arguments against why there's no emphasis on the beauty of Puerto Rican cuisine. Puerto Ricans don't tend to be cerebral about their food but rather emotional.

More than 80 percent of food consumed in Puerto Rico is imported. The costs of importing products, especially food, make them more expensive than if they were produced locally. Most of the time, the food is not even good quality because it has lost its freshness during the long shipping to the island! And don't let it be hurricane season while all this is happening. United States citizens made such a fuss over the "pandemic pantry" during COVID. Puerto Ricans' pantries are basically in a perpetual state of survival mode. The pandemic pantry is a lot of folks' *everyday* pantry. And all the inequity of the United States' industrial cookery culture has really left its mark on Puerto Rican cooking. There's not a single word that I could use to define Puerto Rican cuisine. If I were forced to pick one, I'd choose *sofrito*. This herb paste made of culantro, cilantro, tomatoes, garlic, onion, and chiles or other peppers is the bedrock of our cuisine, which is a straightforward, proletariat proposition—something flavorful, hot, and filling to maintain your strength while you work.

We are Taino, Spanish, and African. The peaceful Taino were not native to the Caribbean; much like their enemies, the cannibalistic Caribs, they migrated to the Antilles from South America. Lots of Taino culture still runs through our veins and our vocabulary—words such as *barbecue*, *hammock*, *canoe*, and *iguana*. The Taino presence is still felt on the island of Borinquen. The Taino called the island Borinquen (land of the brave lord), which is why Puerto Ricans call themselves Boricuas to this day. The Spanish renamed it Porto Rico. While the legend of the Jibaro farmer might be one of folklore, the Taino influence lives on.

A genographic study (National Geographic's Genographic Project, 2014) showed that Native American ancestry is higher in Puerto Rico than in any other Caribbean island, and it originated from groups migrating to Puerto Rico from both South and Central America. It also found that the average Puerto Rican has 12 percent Native American, 65 percent West Eurasian (Mediterranean, Northern European, and/or Middle Eastern), and 20 percent sub-Saharan African DNA. What this study really proves is what some of us already knew: You cannot have the creation of Puerto Rican food without the influence of the Taino, Spanish, and the Africans. Many of our ingredients are straight from Africa. But, according to archeological evidence, the Taino of Puerto Rico cultivated several crops contemporaneously with the Incas of Peru and other peoples of the Andean region. I'm never surprised by the similarities between some Puerto Rican and African dishes, but I'm always surprised by the commonalities in preparations of South American recipes. Most of the crops that are associated with Puerto Rico are not even native to the island: sugarcane, rice, coffee, tobacco, coconut, bananas, plantains, and avocados. All those crops came from Central America or with enslaved Africanos, and they were all far more monetarily valuable than whatever crops were being cultivated by the Taino.

In 1898, after almost four hundred years of Spanish colonial rule, Puerto Rico was ceded by Spain to the United States following the Spanish-American War. The colonial reshaping by the United States focused on instantly monetizing the island's year-round fair weather by producing more valuable crops on an industrial scale. Money, money, money, moneyyyy . . . mooooneyyyyy. For decades, experiment stations, as they were called, popped up all over the island, dabbling in plant propagation and determining which crops would fare better in various locations. In 1910, sugarcane planters built an experiment station in Río Piedras (adjacent to San Juan) that was taken over in 1914 by the United States–enforced Board of Commissioners of Agriculture. This station was of considerable importance in plant introduction work with the creation of the Jones Act and the Merchant Marine Act of 1920, which imposed onerous restrictions on domestic maritime trade. And because most things (water, produce, medicine) come to Puerto Rico via ship, the Jones Act was spilling out of people's mouths during Hurricane Maria. It was an act that fucked with how things work in Puerto Rico long before the devastating hurricane.

The Jones act requires that any vessel engaged in the commercial transportation of goods between two ports within the United States be (a) owned by U.S. citizens and (b) registered under U.S. flag. To be registered under U.S. flag, a vessel must be built, although not maintained or refurbished, in the United States. However, under the Tariff Act of 1930, if a vessel undergoes maintenance or repairs under non-emergency situations in a foreign country, the United States imposes a 50 percent duty on the work performed abroad. Additionally, the U.S.–flag registry requirement triggers another law that requires the U.S.–built vessels to be staffed by a crew primarily consisting of U.S. citizens.

In short, the Act has four basic requirements for a vessel engaged in coastwise trade: that it be (1) owned by the United States, (2) built in the United States, (3) repaired in the United States, unless the carrier is willing to pay the tariff penalty, and (4) crewed by citizens of the United States. The historic justification for these onerous restrictions touches on both national security and commercial interests. Hell, most of the grocery-store chicken sold for consumption in the United States doesn't have to follow these strict guidelines (a lot of that chicken is bred in the United States, processed overseas, and then flown back to be sold in stores)! How the fuck are you gonna impose these restrictions on an island in the middle of the ocean and not on rubbery-ass, frozen, Super Bowl chicken wings?

Besides its politics, another colonial reshaping took place when the United States occupied Puerto Rico: new dietary habits. United States' comestibles made such an impression on generations of Puerto Ricans that cheddar cheese and ketchup would appear in places they had no business turning up, like on top of pasteles—our traditional tamale-like dumplings made of green bananas, plantains, sometimes yuca, sometimes rice, and always filled with a slow-cooked meat stew. I don't eat ketchup on my pasteles, which take hours to make and require multiple hands. It could possibly be one of Puerto Rico's oldest precontact recipes. I can never figure out why anyone would want to ruin that hard work and the essence of a pastel by squeezing ketchup on top—a sort of colonial Stockholm syndrome.

My grandparents came to Sacramento from Puerto Rico in 1956. So, my grandma didn't adopt many of the gastronomic influences that the United States had on Puerto Rico; if we had ever added ketchup to her pasteles, she'd have lost her fucking mind. Many people ask, "Why'd your family choose the West Coast/California/Sacramento?" Like other Puerto Ricans during the great migration in the 1950s, my grandparents left the island to seek bigger opportunities. (There were also rumors about my grandpa's decision to split from the island; political tensions were mounting during a nationalist movement for independence.) Unlike most Puerto Ricans, they bypassed the East Coast. A great deal of my nana's family lived in Philly, including her sister, my titi Rosa. (According to Titi Rosa, she and my grandpa dated each other for a while. How they broke up and he decided to marry her fourteen-year-old sister, my nana, is a little foggy.) Anyway, why would he want to move to a place where some of his skeletons lie? While the information about the familial love triangle is direct from Titi Rosa's mouth (may she rest in peace), the rest is my own theory.

My mother, Carmen (my mami), was three years old when my grandparents arrived Stateside, landing along the muddy banks of the Sacramento River. They bought a house in Oak Park, a historically diverse neighborhood that is now undergoing aggressive gentrification. They lived parallel lives to the Mexicanos with whom they worked the fields and lived alongside. And soon our food and language came to reflect that. My grandma would make handmade tortillas and menudo on Sunday mornings, and I never questioned the Puerto Rican-ness of her cooking.

At 3:55 on an April morning in 1981, when the thick fog made its advectional creep into the valley, leaving the grand oak trees mere silhouettes, I was born at Sutter Memorial Hospital (now demolished) in Sacramento. I grew up in a tiny one-bedroom casita on the corner of 37th and Wilkinson in the Avondale neighborhood (now also demolished) of South Sacramento. My generation rode bikes, gambled Pogs, smoked candy cigarettes, played in fields, drank Clearly Canadians, found food stamps on the street, wore acid-wash overalls (with one strap up and one strap down), and bought cigarettes for our elders with handwritten permission notes. All of it was okay as long as your ass was on the porch by the time the streetlights came on. If I heard Mami's two-finger whistle reverberate on the horizon, it was too

Oak tree, Rancho Llano Seco, Butte County, California.

Northern California foothills.

Piglets, Rancho Llano Seco, Butte County, California.

late for redemption. Famously, she told me, "Whether you're five minutes late or an hour late, it's the same ass whoopin', so make it count."

If you don't know much about Sacramento, there isn't much to tell. It's the capital of California. A cultural wasteland. A dust-bucket town that may give birth to creative types but doesn't nurture them. And it's only a matter of time before they must flee or fail. One of the greatest things about Sacramento is its surrounding bounty of fertile farmland where some of the nation's best produce flourishes. The area grows 80 percent of the world's almonds and 100 percent of the United States' commercial almond supply. The dusty backroads of Northern California are emblazoned in my memory. My mom worked the fields when she was young and would later become a nut sorter on the processing line for Almond Growers, a company now known as Blue Diamond. I consider myself lucky that I know how almonds are harvested. (A machine shakes the shit out of the trees, bringing the nuts to the ground, where they're raked into rows and scooped up by a "pick-up" machine.) Above all, I'm fortunate to have grown up with some of the most beautiful crops in the world readily accessible in my backyard—persimmons, walnuts, pomegranates, oranges, Meyer lemons, grapes, wild blackberries, and more.

Sacramento is promoted as one of the most diverse cities in the nation, but it's incredibly segregated. I did not grow up in the *Lady Bird* version of Sacramento. I did not grow up on the wide tree-lined avenues of Midtown or the Fabulous

Peach blossoms, Twin Oaks Farm, Placer County, California

Forties, as the neighborhood of grand homes east of downtown are called. I grew up in the unincorporated county of South Sacramento, a place that often feels forsaken. It was a neighborhood where you could tell what time of year it was by the activities being performed: cluster mailbox break-ins meant it was income-tax-fraud spring, drive-by shootings were for summer, aggravated battery came with autumn, and robbing season ruled winter. It was a working-class part of town consisting of a diverse immigrant population and a dining scene that reflected it. The smell of charred chiles and cooking tortillas and the sound of a wooden pestle pounding against a kruk would escort you on your evening walks home. All smells and ingredients that would inevitably end up in my Californian–Puerto Rican, or Cali-Rican, cooking style.

And that's why this is not a Puerto Rican cookbook. This book is for the Diasporicans—the 5.5 million people living Stateside who continue to cook the food of our homeland. This is for the tribe of Ni De Aquí, Ni De Allá ("not from here, not from there").

Empanada de cetí, El Nuevo Guayabo, Arecibo, Puerto Rico.

Adoquines, Old San Juan, Puerto Rico.

Diasporican pantry provisions.

Longaniza and morcilla plate, El Rancho de Don Nando, Naranjito, Puerto Rico.

Cooking Traditions and Flavors

There are a few habits and terms to which our people subscribe. They may be superstitions. They may be cautionary techniques learned along the way from a time when certain procedures were essential due to a lack of refrigeration. Either way, here's why we do what we do . . . and don't do.

Washing Meat

This technique requires a person to run their proteins (fish, chicken, goat, pork, and beef) under the running water of a faucet or partially submerge in water in the sink, essentially giving the protein a bath. Some people will go a step further and use vinegar to "clean the meat real good." The vinegar isn't always a bad idea because it can help to tenderize some of the tougher cuts. And I do rub my poultry with vinegar. Pero, I don't "wash" my meat. However, I do pat it dry with a paper towel so the seasonings can better adhere to it. If you feel like washing your meat is keeping you closer to your ancestors, wash on, Sis.

Washing Rice and Why the 2:1 Ratio Is Bullshit

In California, rice grows in water patties that are fertilized with the shit of migrating birds. Then the rice is processed, polished, and sometimes stored in silos in large facilities. Depending on where you get your rice, it can also contain pebbles and other impurities. I think Puerto Ricans wash their rice for these reasons way more than to remove the starch. It could also be a method that's a holdover from the time when they mostly used short- and medium-grain varieties, which would be ultra-sticky unless you removed some of the starch. I wash my rice twice. I allow running water to pour into the bowl of rice, submerging the grains. I give the rice a couple of swishes with my hand and dump the water from the bowl, using my hands as a sieve to capture any strays—the same way that I watched my mother and grandmother do it. Not all the water will be removed, but when you get ready to add the rice to the cooking vessel, use your hand to add most of it and then drain the remaining water from the bowl. Throw the rest of the rice into the cooking vessel.

And the 2:1 Eurocentric ratio most of y'all have been taught is a fucking lie. I knew it was bullshit when they told me in culinary school, "If you use this ratio, you should be fine." The ratio depends on the type of rice and the texture that each culture prefers. Hell, some Asian people will also tell you it depends on the weather the day that you're cooking the rice.

Soaking the Beans

I don't remember Nana or Mami ever soaking their beans. Not overnight. Not for a few hours. They placed the dry beans, onion, garlic, and ham hock directly into the pot and let simmer for hours. Never once did they remove any of the original liquid (no dumping of the "soaking" liquid allowed).

Frying Sofrito

Most Puerto Ricans tend to add sofrito to the heating oil as the first step of a recipe, just as one might add spices to the oil to allow them to bloom. The pungent sofrito kind of gets lost and subdued along the way in the cooking process. It's my own personal preference to add the sofrito toward the end of cooking because it contains fresh cilantro, and I like that fresh herb flavor to pop! I treat it as I would pesto. Sometimes, if I'm cooking for a Puerto Rican, I'll add the sofrito to the oil for ceremony and toward the end for flavor. Putting the sofrito in first reminds me of the start gun at the Olympics—sofrito is the pop that lets everyone know the event has started. But it's the sofrito added at the end that wins us the gold.

Peeling Guineos and Plátanos

For any recipe, you're always going to peel guineos (unripe green bananas) and plátanos (starchy big bananas) the same way. Removing the peel without wearing gloves might turn your fingers black—you decide whether to glove up. Cut off the stem and the bottom tip. Piercing through the peel down to the flesh but being careful not to pierce the flesh too deeply, drag your knife down the natural grooves of the peel, from top to bottom. Slide your thumb under one of the peel slits, separating the peel from the flesh. You may have to occasionally use your knife to remove the peel. This is a more difficult way to peel them, but it ensures that your guineos and plátanos remain firm.

Another way to peel guineos or plátanos is after soaking them in hot water. Use a pot that you do not care if it becomes discolored, because sometimes the sap of the guineos and plátanos will blacken the edges of the pot as well as your hands. Bring a pot of water to a boil and then turn off the heat. Make the slits in the peels and place, still in the peels, into the pot of hot water and let sit for 5 minutes, then remove and peel. (I think this technique softens the fruit, which I don't like.) My nana and mom never used the hot-water trick; they just peeled the raw fruit and placed the exposed interiors in a bowl of salted water to prevent blackening.

Empanadillas versus Pastelillos

There are hundreds of Puerto Ricans prepared to throw hands if I call empanadillas *empanadas*. But that's what empanadillas are and they originate from the same cuisine. It doesn't take a rocket scientist to take one look at this deep-fried pastry pocket, filled with meat and sometimes crab or a sweet offering, to recognize its Spanish ancestor, the empanada. Depending to whom you speak and on which part of the island, the empanada is called an empanadilla if the dough is sturdier and the decorative seal is rope-style. It's a pastelillo if the dough is delicate and flaky and sealed with fork tines. By the way, it's called a taco if it's trifolded like a letter. There's also a puff pastry dessert that has neither a rope- nor a tine-seal that is called pastelillo de guayaba.

And if you were my Puerto Rican grandma living in Sacramento during the 1950s, you would just use a tortilla in place of the dough and deep-fry it for your own version of a taco. Although that would be called a chimichanga. I don't pretend to understand these things. Much like if you're trying to flex that one year of high school Spanish you took and order "salchichas" from a Puerto Rican food stand or restaurant, you will not receive sausages but rather Vienna sausages. Oh, Puerto Ricans.

Puerto Rican Flavor Lexicon

It's hard for me to wax poetic about the seasonings and ingredients that are the workhorses of the Puerto Rican flavor lexicon. (I know, me having a hard time babbling?) To those who are unfamiliar with Puerto Rican food, these seasonings and ingredients might appear unremarkable. Yet, most Puerto Rican dishes would cease to be recognized without the following essential components, most of which go into a good chunk of the savory dishes of Puerto Rico, appearing differently and developing diverse flavor nuances in each of them. The red sauce in a fricassee (usually a light broth made with white wine), for example, is going to be entirely different than the red sauce in a guisada (braised for hours until the tomato sauce deepens in both color and flavor).

ACHIOTE OIL

For a long time, I've been researching whether Africanos combined achiote with oil in an attempt to re-create something similar to the palm oil they used back home, or if achiote oil was simply a replica of the Spanish practice of adding azafran saffron to their cooking. Either way, achiote oil gets a workout during the holidays as the old-fashioned way of giving our iconic foods their orange hue. It makes an appearance in almost all our celebratory Christmas dishes. We use it to season and color pernil and lechón. We pour it on banana leaves before we spoon on the masa for pasteles; the oil also ensures that the masa doesn't stick to the leaves. If watching beans cook was my first kitchen task as a child, my second task was watching achiote seeds sizzle and dance in a pot of manteca, making sure they didn't burn. (Ask any Puerto Rican about burning the achiote seeds. We all have a story.) If you don't want to use the lard, you can use canola or olive oil, and the achiote oil will be more shelf-stable.

ALCAPARRADO

Capers are called *alcaparras* in Spanish, right? Alcaparrado is a mixture of olives, pimientos, and capers sold together in one jar, and it's my worst enemy. (Yes, I am an olive hater—it's a textural thing for me.) But alcaparrado is extremely helpful when you want to double the pungent brine power in a dish.

MAYOKETCHUP

Mayoketchup seems to be the newly chosen sauce for dipping frituras. I'm not a huge fan of ketchup . . . or mayonnaise. But I do agree that sometimes things such as tostones need a dip. I doctor the usual apathetic combo of the two condiments by adding both fresh and dried garlic (fresh gives the punch, dry coats your mouth) and lemon to brighten everything up.

PIQUE

People often ask if Puerto Rican food is spicy. It isn't. But pique is. Pique is a rustic hot sauce you might find on home and restaurant tables; it's spicy from chiles and sharp from vinegar. Pique is often necessary when Puerto Rican food can seem heavy or cumbersome. (Hello, double starch and meat.) When my orange and tangerine trees are heavy with fruit, I replace the pineapple chunks in my recipe with 1 cup of orange or tangerine juice.

SAZÓN AND ADOBO

Sazón and adobo seco (the dry kind of adobo versus the wet mojado marinade version of adobo) are the constantly present paternal twins in our kitchens. Somehow this sibling pop-duo silently crossed over into the non–Puerto Rican kitchen via a big-name corporation's foods, lending their instant MSG-flavor boost to convenient packaging. It wasn't until 2020 that the two truly made some noise when politically conscious folks started to draw a line in the sand on whether to support a corporation that had been single-handedly making hard-to-find products accessible to the nation's second-largest Latin population—Puerto Ricans. It was then that some people wanted to start creating their own sazón and adobo at home.

I don't add any salt to my sazón or adobo because I like to control where the salt goes. (Plus, it's a healthier version for Mami.) Every Puerto Rican has their own sazón and adobo recipes, if they don't use a store-bought variety. Most prefer the sazón combination that contains culantro and achiote. Some people put turmeric in their homemade sazón, attempting to emulate the orange hue that's so quintessential in Puerto Rican cooking. Turmeric in sazón is not the way, y'all. Its musty flavor can be overpowering and is best left for adobo. I never used adobo much as a seasoning until I created my blend. Now I use it on everything from taco meat to Thanksgiving turkey.

SOFRITO

Sofrito is the soul of Puerto Rican cooking—a fuerte herb base that starts (and ends) almost every savory recipe in the card file. Over time, cubanelle and other chile peppers took the place of sweet ají dulces (known in Puerto Rico as ajicitos). If you live in a place where you have access to a wide variety of peppers, use them!

Ají dulces are impossible to find on the West Coast, but I often use gypsy, banana, or other sweet peppers instead when they're in season. Widely available cilantro has come to take the place of culantro. Culantro (also known in Puerto Rico as recao) is used in Latin American and Southeast Asian cooking and is also called sawtooth and long-leaf cilantro. How do you describe culantro's flavor? Culantro is like cilantro's cousin who comes to visit from the hood. Yeah, they're family. But it's also way more "punchy," "vocal," "spirited"—all those politically correct euphemisms—and possibly wearing FUBU. Someone who did not come to play and who gives zero fucks. And yet, you're still happy it showed up to the party because it has the charisma to pull everyone onto the dance floor.

THE RED SAUCE

Let's talk about red sauce. If Puerto Rican cuisine had "mother sauces," red sauce would definitely be one of them. Or maybe the only one. This combination of canned or fresh tomato sauce and sofrito shows up in almost every recipe, and it somehow tastes different in every application. While Puerto Rican cuisine has a massive combination of ingredients when it comes to compound rice dishes, this sauce is the base for most of them. And when you add various proteins—seafood, pork, beef—the result will be different.

Canned tomato sauce lends itself endlessly in the Puerto Rican kitchen, although I have been known to use fresh tomatoes during the summer months. I also use tomato sauce in barbecue sauces, stir-fries, and braises. It adds an unmatched viscosity to ground turkey and ground taco fillings, lending moisture and flavor in short periods of time. Tomato sauce is so important and versatile in Puerto Rican cuisine that we found several dozen cans of it while cleaning out my grandma's kitchen after she passed away.

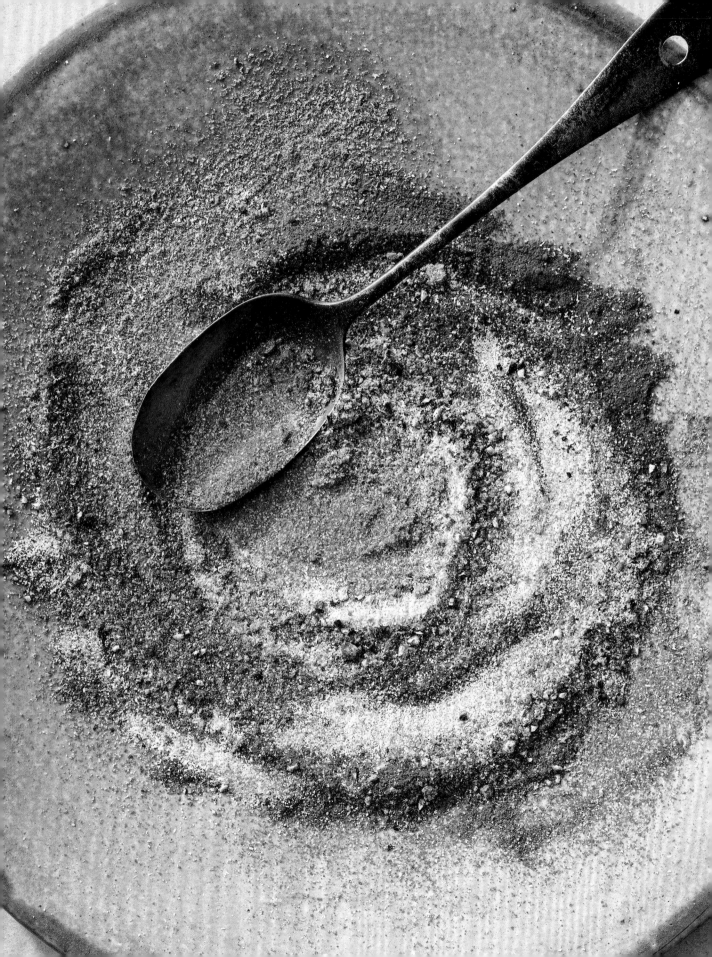

Lexicon Recipes

Don't overlook or underestimate the importance of the combination of just a few simple ingredients or components. Without them, there would be no Puerto Rican food. Achiote oil, sazón, adobo, and sofrito are the workhorses of Puerto Rican cuisine. Most Puerto Ricans would probably say that if an entrée isn't made with a certain meat, then it couldn't possibly be Puerto Rican food; but as long as you include one (or a mixture) of the following components, you could turn any dish into a Puerto Rican offering.

ACHIOTE OIL

Makes 2 cups

2 cups manteca, canola oil, or vegetable oil
½ cup achiote seeds

In a small saucepan over high heat, melt the manteca. Set a mesh sieve over a bowl and place near the stove. As soon as the manteca has melted, carefully add the achiote seeds; they will sizzle. Heat the seeds for 30 seconds to 1 minute, extracting as much of their color and flavor as you can. Never take your eyes off them—they will burn in a blink! When the oil has reached the desired redness, pour it and the seeds through the sieve. Trash the seeds.

If you're using manteca, the achiote oil needs to be used right away. If you're using canola or vegetable oil, pour the cooled achiote oil into a jar with a tight-fitting lid. Store at room temperature for up to 1 year.

ALL-PURPOSE SAZÓN

Makes 10 tablespoons

¼ cup ground achiote
1 tablespoon ground cumin
3 tablespoons granulated garlic
2 tablespoons granulated onion
1 teaspoon freshly ground black pepper

In an airtight container, mix together the achiote, cumin, granulated garlic, granulated onion, and pepper. Store in a cool place for up to 6 months.

ALL-PURPOSE ADOBO

Makes a scant ¼ cup

2 tablespoons granulated garlic
2 teaspoons dried oregano
1 teaspoon ground turmeric
1 teaspoon coarsely ground black pepper

In an airtight container, mix together the granulated garlic, oregano, turmeric, and pepper. Store in a cool place for up to 6 months.

ILLYANNA'S ADOBO

Makes ½ cup

¼ cup Mrs. Dash Original seasoning blend
2 tablespoons granulated garlic
1 tablespoon ground turmeric

In an airtight container, mix together the Mrs. Dash, granulated garlic, and turmeric. Store in a cool place for up to 6 months.

MAYOKETCHUP

Makes 1 cup

1 garlic clove
½ tablespoon granulated garlic
¼ teaspoon coarsely ground black pepper
¾ cup mayonnaise
¼ cup ketchup
½ teaspoon lemon juice

If you're using a pilón, mash the garlic clove until it becomes a paste. Or, using a knife, smash the garlic clove and mince it as finely as possible. Place the fresh garlic in a bowl, add the granulated garlic, and stir to combine. Add the pepper, mayonnaise, and ketchup and stir to combine well, then stir in the lemon juice. Store in the fridge until ready to serve, or for up to 1 week.

PIQUE

Makes 3 cups

½ cup distilled white vinegar

½ cup pineapple vinegar

1 cup frozen pineapple chunks
or orange or tangerine juice

½ cup water

1 habanero chile

1 jalapeño chile

1 cubanelle chile

4 culantro leaves, or 12 cilantro sprigs

6 garlic cloves

3 tablespoons achiote oil (see page 19)

Kosher salt

Freshly ground black pepper

In a blender, combine both vinegars, the
pineapple chunks, water, all the chiles,
culantro, garlic, and achiote oil and blitz
until smooth and thoroughly blended.
Season with salt and pepper. Pour into
a glass bottle and seal with a cap or cork.
Store in the fridge for up to 3 weeks.

SOFRITO

Makes 2 cups

2 Roma tomatoes, quartered

1 yellow onion, quartered

6 garlic cloves, smashed

1 green bell pepper, quartered

1 bunch cilantro, coarsely chopped

1 bunch culantro, coarsely chopped

In a blender, process the tomatoes until finely
chopped. Add the onion and garlic and process
until finely chopped and incorporated. Add the
bell pepper, cilantro, and culantro and process
until the mixture is well combined and mostly
smooth.

You can use the sofrito immediately, cover it
and store in the refrigerator for up to 1 day, or
pour it into an ice-cube tray and freeze for up
to 6 months.

Produce

Puerto Rico is known for its plethora of oranges, mangoes, plantains, bananas, avocados, pana, and coconut. Some of them grow wild or in people's backyards. Hardly any of these are native to Borinquen. When the Spanish arrived in the late 1400s, the only fruit on the island were guava, mamey sapote, papaya, and pineapple, and even some of these were brought from South America by the Taino.

The Spanish did bring in quite a few crops to be cultivated. But, within three years after Spain ceded Puerto Rico to the United States in 1898, multiple Tropical Agriculture Research Stations—like the one in Mayagüez—were installed all over the island to develop genetic diversity within existing crops and to see which ones would be monetarily advantageous for importation, with hyper-focus on cultivars of sorghum, cacao, and beans. The United States wasted no time sucking up the natural resources and utilizing the year-round warm weather to plant more crops.

ACHIOTE

Achiote is also known as annatto. Achiote is a seed native to South America, Mexico, the Caribbean, and Central America that has been extracted and processed since pre-Columbian times for its musky smell, nutty flavor, and food-coloring capabilities. At the turn of the twentieth century, Puerto Rico had five recognized varieties of annatto: pelon, colorado, amarillo, blanco, and negro. Some of the varieties were propagated for selective breeding, which brought in more money via general distribution. Just as achiote is the signature ingredient in the slow-roasted and luxurious Yucatán dish known as cochinita pibil, it is also used in Puerto Rico's famous spit-roasted lechón. It's achiote oil that prevents the pastele masa from sticking to the boiling equipment. And it's used in sazón, which goes into . . . everything.

AJÍ DULCE

These sweet, not spicy, little chiles are a classic component of sofrito. They are ridiculously hard to find on the West Coast. The good news is that I can find a few acceptable substitutes, like gypsy, cubanelle, and banana, at the farmers' market.

APIO

Arracacha, native to the Andes, is also known as *apio* in Puerto Rico. It is said that the Italians gave it that name because of its resemblance in flavor to celery. The tuber itself is squat, gnarled, and beige. Sometimes there's a lilac streak on the base of the stalks, leading into elongated celery-colored stalks and leaves with a yellowish interior. The name *arracacha* was incorporated into Spanish, derived from the Quechua word *raqacha*. Since 1998, one of the largest apio festivals takes place in Barranquitas, Puerto Rico. Apio can be treated much the same as you would a potato.

AVOCADO

For as much as Puerto Ricans love avocados, you'd think the fruit (technically a berry!) was native to the island of Borinquen. Nope. But that doesn't stop customers from requesting a side of avocado, and that doesn't stop the servers at the fondas from bringing those customers a whole-ass avocado and a knife.

BATATA

As early as 1908, the United States started to propagate varieties of sweet potato from already existing ones in Puerto Rico—which were probably being cultivated by the Tainos. Although there is a sweet potato named Porto Rico, which was cultivated and introduced in 1966 by North Carolina State University via propagation from a heritage variety of orange-fleshed sweet potato, this is not the batata that you'll find most Puerto Ricans eating. The widely consumed batatas of La Isla are the orange-fleshed mameya and batata amarilla, which have a pale-yellow interior and ultra-sweet flesh.

CALABAZA

At one time, there was an unknown number of varieties of calabaza in Puerto Rico. The reason these pumpkins were unknown is because people didn't really control their crops—which just grew wild and would crossbreed. What studies have found is that the original calabazas that came to the island were very likely brought from Central or South America. The pumpkins and squashes that we often see Stateside listed as kabocha are the most similar to the type of calabaza found in Puerto Rico. Hell, maybe it's the same kind. It's starchy and the skin is damn near impossible to penetrate. (However, if you cook kabocha for a long time, the skin becomes tender and edible.) Calabaza can be found in various dishes, such as sancocho (see page 68), beans, fritters, and even in pasteles.

CHAYOTE

Native to Mexico and South America, many authors and scientists have long considered chayote indigenous to Puerto Rico and much of the rest of the West Indies. It's possible that the Tainos called chayote by its indigenous name, tayote, but it was Castilianized once the Spanish conquered the island. Chayote is also known as *mirliton* in the American South.

CHINA

Oranges are called chinas (pronounced chee-nahs) in Puerto Rico. They are the same varieties that the Spanish also brought to Florida. Orange groves can be found in the mountainous regions of the island, sometimes alongside coffee trees. In November, small oranges with a brush of green on the outside start to appear in large sacks at many roadside fruit stands. There's no better place to get a sense of this than at the Festival de la China Dulce in Las Marías, where, like most of the food-centric festivals in Puerto Rico, you get a taste of the regional specialties that you wouldn't be able to try anywhere else. At this festival, you'll find a plethora of orange coladas, orange cakes, orange jams, orange juices, and, the regional specialty, polvorones de china, which are orange-scented shortbread cookies. Rumor has it that oranges are called *chinas* because the produce boxes in which they were delivered were labeled "China."

CULANTRO

Originally from South America and Mexico, culantro is native to continental tropical America and the West Indies. Also known as *recao* in Puerto Rico, culantro grows wild in fields and alongside roads and has a concentrated cilantro flavor. Its elongated bright-green leaves have sawtooth edges, and its stalks resemble dandelion greens. Culantro is becoming more available in Southeast Asian markets.

GANDULES

In 1884, it was documented that a single pigeon pea seed was found in an Egyptian burial vault (2400–2200 BCE), along with barley, wheat, pomegranate, lentils, and two broad bean seeds. This reopened the debate over whether the true origin of pigeon peas was Africa versus India. But, because of India's vast array of the *Atylosia* and *Cajanus* species, some have referenced this when speculating about its Indian origin. The conclusion is that the pigeon pea was probably carried from

India to Africa and then from Africa to the Americas. Even if we can't pinpoint where the pigeon pea originated, we can safely assume that it got to Puerto Rico via Africa. The most common gandules in Puerto Rico are the green ones (they turn brown after being cooked), but I've also seen white, purple, and red.

GARBANZOS

Although garbanzos (also known as chickpeas) are frequently used in traditional Puerto Rican recipes, no garbanzos seem to be grown on the island because, historically, their cultivation has failed. All the garbanzos used in Puerto Rico are imported.

GUINEOS

When I reference guineos, I mean guineos verdes, or green bananas. The kind of Dole Cavendish bananas that you buy in the grocery store, but before they turn yellow—the greener, the better. I used to be able to find these only at a little international market in Sacramento; now that fruit is shipped underripe and sold in chain supermarkets, you can find these year-round just about everywhere, especially at Mexican markets. Guineos are not the same as plantains. Rumor has it that the term *guineo* came from bananas originating from Guinea in West Africa. Guineos and plantains are a huge part of the Puerto Rican diet, and they came directly from Africa.

PAJUILES

Pajuil, the Taino name for cashew, is still used today. The fruit (apple) is typically used in juices, while the nut (which is really a seed) must be cooked or roasted. It's toxic if eaten raw.

PANA

It is said that there are two varieties of pana, or breadfruit, in Puerto Rico: pana (seedless) and pana de pepita (with seeds). There's some evidence that a French dude named Pierre Sonnerat spotted the latter while he was in the Philippines in the late 1700s. It was Sonnerat who brought the breadnut (pana de pepita, which is spiky and contains seeds that look like chestnuts) to the French West Indies. From there, it quickly made its way to Jamaica via the British, who had captured a French boat carrying breadfruit. By 1784, two plants of pana de pepita were documented in Jamaica. This is how pana could have made it to the other islands in the Caribbean. It's also widely known that Captain William Bligh set out on a trip in 1791, delivering hundreds of potted seedless breadfruit plants to Jamaica

on his "floating forest" of a boat containing hordes of other plants—sort of a nautical version of a door-to-door salesman with breadfruit stolen from Tahiti and sold to other islands. And this is how Puerto Rico could have gotten its smooth, seedless pana.

PLÁTANOS AND AMARILLOS

Big, starchy green bananas, plátanos are more like a vegetable than fruit. You'll know plátanos when you see them because they are often sold individually (rather than grouped together like the familiar yellow Cavendish bananas) and are considerably larger. When they're green, they're called plátanos verdes. When they're yellow, they're called amarillos. When green plátanos are smashed and fried, they're called tostones. When the amarillos are fried, they're called maduros. When the two are mashed and molded into a mound, they're called mofongo (or bifongo). Straight to Puerto Rico from Africa.

Because of the way the States exposes bananas to ethylene gas to ripen them, sometimes the fruit will be bright green but already soft on the inside. The same goes for the plátanos. Sometimes plátanos can take a month to ripen, and sometimes they don't ripen at all. This is not what you want. Recently, I've been using what's labeled as *Hawaiian plantains*. They're more squat than the plátanos that I'm accustomed to, but there seems to be no difference in flavor or textural outcome.

QUENEPA

This squishy-fleshed, extraterrestrial-like orb of sourness is ripe and ready in summer months, even in the year-round tropical climate of Puerto Rico. If you combine a few quenepas in a bottle with sugar, vanilla extract, and some warming spices, it becomes bilí, or, more specifically, bilí de quenepas, which is a rustic alcoholic creation. Try finding quenepas on the West Coast. Impossible!

UVA DE PLAYA

I've consumed sea grapes only once and it was in a rustic pique. But the leathery leaves of the plant can be found in the hands of almost every beachside kiosk vendor who uses the leaves' sturdiness to form the crunchy deep-fried fritters known as alcapurrias.

YAUTÍA

For decades, there has been a debate about whether yautía and malanga are the same thing. In a 1905 article, "The Yautias, or Taniers, of Porto Rico" by Otis Warren Barrett, several professors argued whether malanga is a "false yautía" and whether its name is West African or a genuine Arawak word. While they decided it was an Arawak word, they never settled the debate on whether malanga and yautía are identical. These starchy tubers come in white, yellow, and purple with hard interiors that are similar in texture to yuca. Although they have rough, brown exteriors, much like a coconut, with lots of hairs, you can peel them like a potato. I have heard from many traditional Puerto Rican wela cooks that what we call "yautía" in Puerto Rico, grocers label as "malanga" Stateside. Only one place in my hometown sells it labeled as yautía. But there are plenty of Asian markets that sell malanga. When you look at malanga and yautía . . . they appear the same. When you cook malanga and yautía, they cook the same; they act the same when I interchangeably use them in my pasteles. And when you eat malanga and yautía, they taste the same. I'm just gonna leave it at that.

YUCA

One of the primary crops cultivated by the Taino was yuca (pronounced YOU-ca), or cassava. Tainos praised the god Yucahu as the giver of yuca. They would process yuca into flour, extracting all the poisonous water from it, and turn the flour into a flatbread known as casabe. Then they'd cook the flatbread on flat stones called burénes, a prequel to the large metal burén. Casabe was mentioned in Columbus's journal as something the crew stocked on their ship for the voyage back to Spain. Also, it must be said, I'll die if I have to hear another person say "YUCK-a."

Equipment

Here are several simple tools you will find in a Puerto Rican kitchen. Even if some of these have been given up in the name of modernity—the colador replaced with a coffeepot, the pilón replaced with a blender—Puerto Ricans still have them, for the nostalgia.

CALDERO

Bare aluminum pots are quintessential Puerto Rican cookware—an iconic symbol. These pots can withstand incredibly high temperatures, conduct heat more evenly, and require minimal upkeep. It's the only type of pot that I use for my rice dishes so they turn out perfectly. I find that if you cook Puerto Rican compound rice in any other type of vessel, it tends to be amogollao. I inherited my nana's blackened calderos when she passed away; they were the only thing of hers that I wanted.

COLADOR

Before pour-overs became an excuse to add an extra buck to your coffee routine, Puerto Ricans had "the sock." A colador is a cloth strainer, attached to a wooden handle, into which coffee grounds are spooned and hot water is poured over, creating a pure and strong coffee. With no access to a colador in Sacramento, one time I think I saw my grandma use pantyhose.

PILÓN

The pilón is a wooden mortar and pestle used to make and serve mofongo, as well as mash garlic and chiles. The original pilóns were made from hollowed-out tree trunks and subsequently waist-high. Today, pilóns vary from simplistic and utilitarian to elaborate works of art. There are still craftsmen on the island, like the Rivera brothers in Morovis, not too far from my family in Vega Baja, who are making these by hand. They are commonly made from caoba (mahogany) or guayacán wood.

TOSTONERA

A tostonera is exactly what it sounds like—a tool to make tostones. It's a press that's usually made from wood, sometimes plastic, that flattens thick plantain slices, turning them into thin discs to be fried. A tortilla press also works.

Frituras

Frituras simply means "fritters." A celebratory meal will often begin with a few of these fried treats, like a small pastelillo or alcapurria. The reason some of the best frituras can be found at various beachside kiosks in Loíza is because the frying technique is directly descended from Africa, and Loíza was one of the first places where enslaved Africans set up a community. These fritters can be found glowing underneath heat lamps, but the best kiosks serve them up fresh, accompanied by an ice-cold Medalla—Puerto Rico's answer to Budweiser. My grandmother would always start our celebratory meals with bacalaitos, fritters made from bacalao (salted and dried cod).

My maternal great-grandma, Abuela Emilia, was born in Puerto Rico around 1913 and died in 2003, when she was about ninety. We knew nothing about each other. Hell, I didn't even know I had a great-grandma until we showed up on her stoop in North Philly in 1996. My mother and I had agreed to a temporary cease-fire long enough to endure a trip to Philadelphia together. I was fifteen. My mom was forty-three. I was going through teenage angst. My mom was going through menopause. We brought along my mom's youngest sister as a much-needed buffer. Teenagers test the waters of independence by flying farther and farther away from the nest, developing their own identities and honing their craft as professional liars. I was no exception. For the first time in my childhood, I was alone a lot. I was lonely. I had no cousins around to protect me or speak up for me for the first time ever. Mom was working twelve-hour shifts, so I hardly saw her. The only friend that I had since middle school turned against me in high school and led a bullying campaign (which involved handing me a razor and a bar of soap in the hallway to "shave my beard"). I tried to go live with my father

Opposite, background: Granitos de Humacao. Opposite, inset, clockwise from top left: Bacalaitos, Guichis, Empanadillas, Arepas with Ensalada de Pulpo y Camarones, Pastelillo, Arepas.

but found out that fool already had a whole other family and was pretending I had never been born. I was just trying to figure it out on my own, until the cops showed up at our door and told my mom that I had missed months of school and they were going to send her to jail if I didn't get my shit together.

As soon as we walked into my great-grandma's three-story, brick row house, she disappeared into the kitchen. I followed her and sat on a stool underneath an archaic wall-mounted phone, my new yellow Perry Ellis windbreaker blending in with the yellow floral wallpaper. Emilia started cooking bacalaitos. She ran her hands through the soaked cod fillets that sat in an oversize enamel bowl until they broke into tiny pieces. She added flour, a splash of water, and a little baking powder and then swirled the batter around with her hand. Displeased with the texture, she added a little more water. This dance went on until she deemed the mixture a good consistency. She took a large spoonful of the snow-white batter and placed it into the hot, glistening oil in a cast-iron skillet. After seconds went by, she flipped it. She turned to me and handed me the first bacalaito out of the frying pan. Her mahogany hands were gnarled like ancient grapevines, and her eyes, turned down in the corners, told chapters of trauma. Emilia's bacalaitos were golden, and the edges resembled the celebrated mundillo lace of Moca.

Before you even taste the flavor of a bacalaito, you hear the crunch. The shatter. The center was toothsome like our gente's—our people's—resistance, salty from the tears we've shed, but the edges were delicate and vulnerable, like when we reveal our underbellies. Abuela Emilia's bacalaito was also familiar. I had eaten it before because it was my nana's bacalaito. They hadn't seen each other in forty years, but their identical bacalaitos proved they were still connected. Whether they liked it or not.

I realized in that moment that my mom had molded her life in my best interest. Ensuring I didn't become a statistic. Ensuring I didn't have to face the same traumas she did, the traumas that force so many of our gente to grow up before their time. So, when I was sent to continuation school and I had failed, she took it personally. Maybe she felt that she had failed. It's been nearly twenty years since I made those mistakes, and I still haven't forgiven myself. Good old-fashioned residual penance.

Frying bacalaitos, Loíza, Puerto Rico.

Bacalaitos

Makes about 8 fritters

The whole process of soaking and draining the bacalao is to remove its saltiness. However, I prefer the salinity, so I don't spend a lot of time soaking and draining. I'm not even sure that I remember my nana soaking bacalao either. Instead, I submerge it in cold water and bring to a slow simmer until it flakes. Then I drain it. But, if the bacalao is still too salty, rinse and repeat until it's to your liking; for the sake of this recipe, I'm going to include the soaking method. Bacalao can sometimes be hard to find. If you can't find it at a local store, you can always order it online.

14 ounces bacalao

1½ cups all-purpose flour

1 teaspoon baking powder

Canola oil or vegetable oil for frying

Kosher salt

Submerge the bacalao in a large bowl of water, cover, and let soak overnight at room temperature. Discard the soaking water.

Fill a pot with 3 cups water and place over medium heat. When the water is warm, submerge the bacalao, bring to a simmer, and let simmer for about 30 minutes, until the fish easily tears apart with your fingers. Break the bacalao into small pieces, as finely as possible, and place in a bowl. Set the bowl aside and reserve the cooking water, letting it cool completely.

In a separate mixing bowl, combine the flour and baking powder. Gradually add about 2½ cups of the reserved water and mix until it reaches a smooth, loose, pancake-batter consistency. Add the bacalao and mix again.

Line a plate with paper towels and set near the stove. Fill a 10-inch cast-iron skillet with ½ inch of canola oil and place over medium-high heat. You want enough oil to slightly cover the fritters. Heat the oil until it registers 350°F on an instant-read thermometer. (Sprinkle in a little flour; if the oil sizzles, it's ready for frying.)

Spoon ½ cup of the batter into the pan and fry for 2 to 5 minutes on one side, until the edges are golden and the middle is still slightly pale. Flip and cook for 4 minutes more. Transfer the bacalaito to the prepared plate and sprinkle with salt while hot. Repeat with the remaining batter.

Serve the bacalaitos immediately.

Note: The tricks to making these are getting the water the right temperature and using the correct amount of oil. If the water is too hot when you add it to the flour, the fritter might turn out gummy. That's why you must let the water cool completely. Use just enough oil to coat the bottom of the pan and reach a little up the sides.

Empanadillas—Pastelillos

Makes 10 servings

The battle of what to call the empanada . . . much like many other things in Puerto Rico, to claim their own (and not cede to the Spanish or Americans), Puerto Ricans call empanadas either empanadillas or pastelillos.

The empanada is mentioned, possibly for the first time in print, in a book originally called *Libre del Coch*, which was published in 1520 and written in Catalan by an author named Mestre Robert, later known as Ruperto de Nola. These recipes would be plagiarized by Diego Granado in his 1599 book *Libro del Arte de Cozina*. During the period in which the book was written, empanadas were a pie made with bread dough, or *en pan*, which translates to "in bread," with top and bottom crusts made of well-sifted white flour, cold water, salt, and a little manteca, whereas pastelillos had a bottom crust made of lard-based pie dough and a top crust of hojaladre, or leaf-pastry. Two different doughs for the empanada and pastelillo. While most people use premade empanada wrappers from the frozen section of the market, the preferred fillings in Puerto Rico are still picadillo (a bracingly flavorful ground beef mixture filled with sofrito and tomato sauce) and jueyes (stewed land crab).

But the evolution of the filling has expanded with the current generation's palate, and now you have tender braised chicken mixed in with melty cheese as well as pizza-inspired versions with pepperoni and . . . melty cheese. The pepperoni fat and the gooey cheese go into the dough as individual ingredients but sync up during the cooking process (which in Puerto Rico is frying). The thick, crusty exterior of the empanadilla encases the combination until you've bitten into its hull and the cheese starts to ooze out like a cephalopodic tentacle. If Mestre Robert and Diego Granado were still alive, I'm sure they'd reach for the camera to capture that cheese pull.

2 1/2 cups all-purpose flour

1 pinch kosher salt

1/2 cup vegetable shortening or manteca

1/2 cup water with 2 ice cubes

1 1/4 cups picadillo (see page 144)

Canola oil for frying

In a large bowl, combine the flour and salt. With the tips of your fingers or a pastry cutter, cut the shortening into the flour. Gradually add the water without letting the ice fall into the bowl. Continue to combine the mixture until it comes together, then knead for a few minutes and form into a disc. Wrap the dough in plastic wrap and chill in the fridge for 15 to 20 minutes.

Flour your work surface and rolling pin. Roll out the chilled dough to 1/8 inch thick. Using a 3-inch round biscuit cutter or mold (sometimes I use the tops of margarine containers), cut the dough into ten circles.

continued ▶

Put 1 to 2 tablespoons picadillo in the center of each dough circle. Bring one side of the circle over to the other side and enclose the filling. With a fork, press the tines all along the crescent seam to seal it closed. Alternatively, you can fold a small section along the crescent seam onto itself, repeating the process to create a rope effect.

Place a wire cooling rack in a baking sheet and set near the stove. Fill a 10-inch cast-iron skillet with 2 inches of canola oil and place over medium-high heat. You want enough oil to slightly cover the empanadillas. Heat the oil until it registers 350°F on an instant-read thermometer. (Sprinkle in a little flour; if the oil sizzles, it's ready for frying.)

Place the filled empanadillas in the hot oil a few at a time and fry for 3 to 5 minutes on each side, until they turn a deep golden brown. Using tongs or a slotted spoon, transfer to the prepared rack.

Serve the empanadillas immediately.

Note: You can substitute store-bought empanada dough, found in the freezer section of your international markets, or use rolled pie crusts, which are sold in the refrigerated section of the market.

Papas Rellenas

Makes 12 (2-inch) rellenas

Also known as relleno de papa, these are potato dumplings stuffed with picadillo and then fried. I happen to have a love affair with instant potatoes. They were one of my mother's go-to semi-homemade secret weapons to get dinner on the table, hot and fast, usually served with her famous "meat and gravy" (ground beef in a quick gravy). Some of you know that cooking has never been her favorite thing—it was simply another chore—and she seldomly made Puerto Rican food. The next day, she'd take the cold potatoes and turn them into papas rellenas. Honestly, no one to whom I have served these could tell the difference.

1 teaspoon canola oil or vegetable oil, plus more for frying

8 ounces ground beef

1 tablespoon sazón (see page 19)

1 teaspoon olive brine

¼ cup sofrito (see page 23)

Kosher salt

Freshly ground black pepper

4 cups instant potato flakes

3 tablespoons cornstarch, or as needed

3 cups water

2 cups panko

In a 10-inch cast-iron skillet over medium heat, warm the 1 teaspoon canola oil. Add the ground beef, sazón, olive brine, and sofrito; season with salt and pepper; and cook for 10 to 15 minutes. Set aside to cool.

In a mixing bowl, combine the instant potato flakes and cornstarch and stir to incorporate. Set aside.

In a medium pot over medium heat, bring the water to a low simmer. Remove from the heat and stir the water into the potato-cornstarch mixture, which should stiffen up instantly. If the mixture seems a little loose (it should be really thick and stiff like lumpy mashed potatoes), gradually add more potato flakes a little at a time. It's impossible to get this mixture too thick. Set aside to cool completely.

Place the panko in a mixing bowl and set it near your stove. Dust your hands with cornstarch. Working as fast as you can, take some of the potato mixture and form a patty the size of your hand. Make a small indention in the middle of the patty and add 1 to 2 tablespoons of the ground beef mixture. Fold the potato mixture over the meat mixture, rotating the patty and encasing the meat until the filling is no longer visible. Drop the potato patty into the panko and gently roll it around to fully coat. Repeat to make four more patties. (The patties can be formed, stuffed, and frozen for up to 3 months. Fry them frozen without thawing.)

Place a wire cooling rack in a baking sheet and set near the stove. Fill a 2-quart pot with 3 inches of canola oil and place over medium-high heat. You want enough oil to slightly cover the rellenas. Heat the oil until it registers 350°F on an instant-read thermometer. (Add a tiny piece of the potato patty; if the oil sizzles, it's ready for frying.)

Transfer the patties to the oil, flipping them with a chopstick or a fork, and cook for about 4 minutes on each side, until golden brown. Using tongs or a slotted spoon, transfer the patties to the prepared rack. Repeat with the remaining potato patties.

Serve the papas rellenas immediately.

Tostones

Makes 4 to 6 servings

To the naked eye, tostones are one of those recipes that seem easy to make, and for the most part they are. But they're also not. You could technically just take green plantains and mash them into flattened discs, but the key to truly magical tostones is soaking them in water. And for the people who do soak, their methods vary; some soak the plátanos in the beginning, some in the middle, and some at the end. If you don't want to make the dipping sauce, just use mayoketchup (see page 20).

2 cups water, at room temperature

1 tablespoon All-Purpose Adobo (page 20)

Kosher salt

2 large plátanos, peeled (see page 12)

Canola oil for frying

Dipping Sauce

4 garlic cloves

¼ cup olive oil

1 tablespoon Dijon mustard

¼ cup lemon juice

Kosher salt

½ bunch parsley, coarsely chopped

In a medium bowl, combine the water and adobo and season with salt. Mix until the adobo and salt dissolve. Set aside. Slice the plátanos into 1-inch-thick chunks.

Line a plate with paper towels and set near the stove. Fill a 10-inch cast-iron skillet with 2 inches of canola oil and place over medium-high heat. You want enough oil to slightly cover the plátanos. Heat the oil until it registers 350°F on an instant-read thermometer. (Add a tiny piece of plátano; if the oil sizzles, it's ready for frying.)

In batches, add the plátano chunks to the oil and fry for 1 to 3 minutes on one side, or until golden brown and softened. Flip them and fry for 1 to 3 minutes more, or until softened. Using tongs or a slotted spoon, transfer the plátanos to the prepared plate to drain. Either turn down the heat or remove the pan from the heat.

Line a tostonera with two pieces of parchment paper. Transfer the fried plátano to the tostonera (one parchment piece should be on the bottom of the plátano and the other piece of parchment on top) and mash to the desired thickness. If you don't have a tostonera, place the plátano chunks between two pieces of parchment paper on a work surface and mash them with the bottom of a drinking glass, cast-iron skillet, plate, or baking sheet. Slide them into the adobo-seasoned water and let soak for 2 to 3 minutes.

Place a wire cooling rack in a baking sheet and set near the stove. Remove the tostones from the water, pat dry with a paper towel, and return them to the frying pan over medium-high heat. Cook for 1 to 3 minutes on one side, flip, and fry for 1 to 3 minutes more, or until crispy and brown. Using tongs or a slotted spoon, transfer the tostones to the prepared rack. Taste and season with salt if needed.

To make the dipping sauce: In a blender or food processor, combine the garlic, olive oil, mustard, and lemon juice; season with salt; and blitz until smooth. Add the parsley and blitz until it is incorporated.

Serve the tostones with the sauce spooned over or for dipping.

Sunset over El Morro, San Juan, Puerto Rico.

Macabeos

Makes 6 servings

As far as I know, macabeos are unique to the town of Trujillo Alto in Puerto Rico. They look like a crescent-shaped alcapurria at first glance, although many Trujillanos will cast the evil eye on you if you even think about comparing macabeos to alcapurrias. The difference between the two is that macabeos are solely made with a combination of raw and cooked guineos—green bananas—that are formed, shaped, stuffed, and deep-fried. Alcapurrias don't contain cooked guineos, only raw. The best place to taste these treats is the annual Macabeo Festival, which has been held in Trujillo Alto every December since the 1980s. Historically, these fritters have been shaped and formed on banana leaves, giving the masa a grassy essence. But, don't worry, you can also use parchment paper or aluminum foil.

9 guineos, peeled (see page 12)

1 tablespoon sazón (see page 19)

¼ cup achiote oil (see page 19), plus 6 tablespoons

1 cup plus 2 tablespoons picadillo (see page 144)

Canola oil for frying

Kosher salt

Place a box grater in a large bowl. Using the side with the smallest holes (the ones that protrude outward and are spiky), grate three of the guineos. You're looking for a smooth purée, not matchstick, texture.

Bring a pot of salted water to a boil over medium-high heat. Add the remaining six guineos and boil for 15 to 20 minutes, or until they are very soft. Transfer the guineos to a mixing bowl. Add the sazón and, using a fork, mash completely while hot. Add the grated guineos to the hot mash, along with the ¼ cup achiote oil, and mix well until it forms a dough that is on the stiff side. This is your masa.

Cut six banana leaves, or parchment paper or aluminum foil, into 12-inch squares. Spoon 1 tablespoon of achiote oil on each square. Using the back of the spoon, spread the oil in a circular motion, pushing it outward to create a larger circle. Scoop ½ cup of the masa onto the achiote-oil circle. The mixture may be stiff, so pat it into a 6-inch circle. Place a heaping 3 tablespoons of picadillo in the center of each circle. Fold one side of the banana leaf over the other, encasing the filling and forming the macabeo into its iconic crescent shape. Repeat to make the remaining macabeos.

Place a wire cooling rack in a baking sheet and set near the stove. Fill a medium pot with about 2 inches of canola oil and place over medium heat. You want enough oil to partially submerge the macabeos. Heat the oil until it registers 350°F on an instant-read thermometer. (Add a tiny piece of the macabeo dough; if the oil sizzles, it's ready for frying.)

Drop three macabeos into the hot oil and fry for 5 to 7 minutes, or until the insides are still a little moist (break one open to check) and the outside is deep brown. Using tongs or a slotted spoon, transfer the macabeos to the prepared rack. Repeat to cook the remaining macabeos.

Sprinkle the macabeos with salt and serve immediately.

Alcapurrias de Jueyes

Makes 18 alcapurrias

Alcapurrias are essentially deep-fried pasteles. They share the same complex and laborious dough, which is why it's sensible to assemble them if you're already making pasteles (see page 128). Alcapurrias are stuffed with a variety of proteins, the most popular (and economical) being ground beef. But you'll often find stewed crab as an option among the beach kiosks in Loíza.

2 pounds Dungeness lump crabmeat

1 tablespoon sofrito (see page 23)

1 tablespoon tomato sauce

1 small lemon

6 guineos, peeled (see page 12)

1 plátano, peeled (see page 12)

1 pound yautía, peeled

½ small russet potato, peeled

1 tablespoon milk

Kosher salt

1½ cups achiote oil (see page 19), or as needed

Canola oil for frying

In a mixing bowl, combine the crabmeat, sofrito, tomato sauce, and a squeeze of lemon juice and stir to mix. Set aside.

Place a box grater in a large bowl. Using the smallest holes of the grater (the ones that protrude outward and are spiky), grate the guineos, plátano, yautía, and potato half. With your hands, combine the vegetables and mix well. Add the milk, season with salt, and mix. Add ¼ cup of the achiote oil and mix again. This is your masa. You want it to be relatively "stained" with oil; stir in more achiote oil if needed.

Cut eighteen banana leaves, or parchment paper or aluminum foil, into 10-inch squares. Spoon 1 tablespoon of the remaining achiote oil on a square. Using the back of the spoon, spread the oil in a circular motion, pushing it outward to create a larger circle. Scoop ½ cup of the masa onto the achiote-oil circle. Place 2 tablespoons of the crab filling in the center of the circle. Dip a spoon in achiote oil and use it to push one side of the masa snugly up against the filling. Repeat with the other side. Keep smoothing the masa until the filling is no longer visible; the goal is to fully enclose the filling with the masa. Repeat to form the remaining alcapurrias.

Place a wire cooling rack in a baking sheet and set near the stove. Fill a medium pot with 2 inches of canola oil and place over medium heat. You want enough oil to partially submerge the alcapurrias. Heat the oil until it registers 350°F on an instant-read thermometer. (Add a tiny piece of the masa; if the oil sizzles, it's ready for frying.)

In batches, slide the alcapurrias off their squares directly into hot oil and fry for 5 to 7 minutes, or until the insides are still a little moist (break one open to check) and the outsides are deep brown. Using tongs or a slotted spoon, transfer to prepared wire rack. Repeat to cook the remaining alcapurrias.

Sprinkle the alcapurrias with salt and serve immediately.

Arañitas de Plátano

Makes 6 patties

Santana is one of my closest friends and he is Ecuadorian. When I asked his mom if she would make some regional specialties from their coastal town, she obliged by making shrimp ceviche in a mustard-ketchup-based sauce, topped with chifles (super-thin plátano chips) and mashed sweet banana fritters with cubes of white cheese and sprinkled with sugar. And here's what blew my mind: shredded green plátano and cilantro nests, placed in a cast-iron skillet and shallow-fried like hash browns. The Ecuadorian version of tortitas de plátano are our arañitas de plátano, step for step and ingredient for ingredient.

1 plátano, peeled (see page 12)
Freshly ground black pepper
1 teaspoon garlic powder
1 teaspoon onion powder
Canola oil for frying
Kosher salt

Place a box grater in a large bowl. Using the largest holes of the grater (the flat ones you'd use to grate cheese), grate the plátano. Season with pepper, the garlic powder, and onion powder and stir to mix. Set aside.

Line a plate with paper towels and set near the stove. Fill a 10-inch cast-iron skillet with ½ inch of canola oil and place over medium heat. You want enough oil to partially submerge the arañitas. Heat the oil until it registers 350°F on an instant-read thermometer. (Add a little of the plátano mixture; if the oil sizzles, it's ready for frying.)

Place palm-size mounds of the plátano shreds in the hot oil and fry for 2 to 5 minutes, until brown and cooked through. Using a slotted spoon, transfer the mounds to the prepared plate.

Sprinkle the arañitas with salt and serve immediately.

Granitos de Humacao

Makes 8 to 10 servings

Mami, my cousin, and I drove from San Juan to Humacao to consume granitos de Humacao at a local granito factory. You can find granitos de Humacao only in . . . Humacao. (And some bordering towns, due to economic migration.) Because of colonialism, there's also very little information on why this is one of the only areas in which to find granitos. All the little rice fritters at the factory are made in-house. "Factory" loosely describes the place. The equipment is in a small room with concrete floors, where women stand around a large food-grade bin filled with rice-flour dough and continuously form the granitos. Rows and rows of uniform fritters sit like soldiers on a stainless-steel work bench. The only sign of what's special about the place is the constant line of people outside and the smell of toasted rice intermingling with the calls of caged roosters across the street.

Some granoderas use processed rice flour, while others grind their own. At the factory I visited, an employee stands between a wall of yellow bags of rice and an antiquated coffee grinder. As the contents of the bags are dumped into the grinder, the staffer's arms accumulate the fine white dust that floats in the air from the process while the machine's grumbling echoes through the factory as it herds the rice flour that will eventually go into boiling water, along with salt and manteca, into white buckets. As the granodera works quickly, the mixture seems to instantaneously tighten up as it's combined using an oversize wooden paddle, resisting, resisting, resisting. The mixing happens until the consistency has tension. Then the masa is patted down into the cooking vessel, and holes are poked into the compacted mixture to allow for even cooling.

Much like a sushi chef who hand-forms rice for nigiri, granoderas form the granito mixture into its iconic shape using primitive hand spatulas. The granito goes down the assembly line: It's formed, placed on the workbench, and receives a minuscule piece of queso de bola (Edam cheese) in the center. Then, only on weekdays, granitos are fried in large vats of oil until golden brown and crispy. The center retains a sort of soft stickiness. The piece of cheese is so small that it seems inessential, but it does provide a salty bite. If the piece of cheese is any bigger, the granito will crack and not hold its shape.

Researching this recipe was the first time that I truly understood that Puerto Rican food could be regional. Granitos haven't appeared in any books or English-language publications. No travel writers know about granitos de Humacao—mostly because none of them has local

continued ▶

connections on the island and because they hardly ever leave the fucking San Juan area! Granitos will appear in people's social feeds from now on.

Because the dough requires a lengthy cooling time before it's formed and fried, you can make it a day ahead, cover with a damp paper towel or kitchen towel, and refrigerate overnight.

4 cups water

Kosher salt

2 tablespoons manteca (see Note) or vegetable shortening

2 to 3 cups rice flour (preferably Faraon or Koda Farms brand)

½ cup diced Edam or Gouda cheese (cut into ¼-inch dice)

Canola oil for frying

In a saucepan over medium-high heat, combine the water, 1 teaspoon salt, and manteca and bring to a rolling boil. Slowly add 2 cups of the rice flour, stirring constantly with a whisk to prevent lumps; add enough of the remaining 1 cup flour to form a dough. When the dough is too thick to stir with the whisk, change to a wooden spoon and keep mixing vigorously. If it starts to bubble and pop, take it off the heat for a few seconds, still stirring, and then return it to the heat for a few seconds, and keep stirring. This will take 3 to 7 minutes; the dough should look like super-thick polenta or grits. Remove the saucepan from the heat.

Using the handle of the wooden spoon, poke holes in the dough and set aside to cool completely; this could take anywhere from 30 minutes to several hours. After the dough has cooled, moisten your hands with water to ensure that the dough doesn't stick to them. Scoop 2 tablespoons of the dough into one hand and form it into the shape of a canoe. Press a piece of cheese into the center of the canoe and shape the existing dough over the cheese until it's completely covered (otherwise the cheese will disintegrate in the cooking oil if left exposed).

Place a wire cooling rack in a baking sheet and set near the stove. Fill a 2-quart pot with 3 inches of canola oil and place over medium-high heat. You want enough oil to fully submerge the granitos. Heat the oil until it registers 350°F on an instant-read thermometer. Place one granito in the oil; if it's fully submerged and sizzling, the oil is ready. It's important to have the oil hot enough to preserve the shape of the granito and ensure that it'll start cooking as soon as it hits the oil.

Gently add just enough of the granitos to the oil to fit without overcrowding and fry for 5 to 7 minutes, or until golden. Using a slotted spoon, transfer the granitos to the prepared rack. Season with salt while hot. Repeat to fry the remaining granitos.

Serve the granitos immediately.

Note: If you bought manteca specifically for this recipe, use the rest of it (instead of canola oil) to fry the granitos.

Almojábanas

Makes 24 almojábanas

These cheesy fritters made from rice flour are believed to date back to the Middle Ages (originally known as *almojavanas* in Catalan), and there are claims that the name derives from *almugábbana*, an Arabic word that translates to "cheese mixture." Some have even said that granitos de Humacao (see page 49) were an evolution of almojábanas. Almojábana vendors can be found in the northwest and central regions of the island—especially in the town of Lares, where the annual Almojábana Festival is held—selling warm fritters at roadside carts to laborers in the early morning.

1 cup milk

3 tablespoons salted butter

1 tablespoon granulated sugar

1½ cups rice flour (preferably Faraon or Koda Farms brand)

2 teaspoons baking powder

2 eggs

¾ cup shredded white cheddar cheese

¼ cup shredded Edam cheese

Kosher salt

Canola oil for frying

In a medium saucepan, combine the milk, butter, and sugar; place over medium heat; and bring to a slow simmer. In a large bowl, combine the rice flour and baking powder. Pour the milk mixture into the bowl and mix well. Add the eggs, one at a time, ensuring that each one is well incorporated before adding the next. Add the cheddar cheese, Edam cheese, and ¼ teaspoon salt and mix to combine.

Place a wire cooling rack in a baking sheet and set by the stove. Fill a 2-quart pot with 3 inches of canola oil and place over medium-high heat. You want enough oil to almost fully cover the almojábanas. Heat the oil until it registers 350°F on an instant-read thermometer. (Add a tiny piece of the almojábana dough; if the oil sizzles, it's ready for frying.)

Scoop a heaping 1 tablespoon of the dough and then use another spoon to help guide it into the hot oil. Repeat to add enough scoops to fit without crowding and fry for 5 to 7 minutes, or until the dough is golden brown. Flip and cook the other side for 3 to 5 minutes more. Using tongs or a slotted spoon, transfer the almojábanas to the prepared rack. Season with salt while hot.

Serve the almojábanas immediately.

Guichis

Makes 5 guichis

Guichis is a relatively new recipe. I came across it one night during a jump down the rabbit hole. Through a reverse research process, I found Myraida Santana. Myraida knew about guichis because her mother, Carmen Morales, made them. I asked Myraida for her mother's contact information, and Carmen shared the story/hearsay/rumor of how guichis came to be, telling me, "Dona Coffa was known to be a strong woman who eventually left her husband and started her own business—a food stand in Corozal." Apparently Coffa invented this recipe on the fly and named it after her son, Luis, affectionately nicknamed Guichi. From there, she built an empire that spanned several generations. Guichis are a simple snack, consisting of only a handful of ingredients. I have never seen it outside the central-eastern region of the island. Thank you to Myraida Santana and Carmen Morales for helping me track down the origins of guichis and for sharing their family's history and recipe! This is my own rendition.

5 small white potatoes, peeled

5 slices good-quality ham

5 slices cheddar cheese

1 cup all-purpose flour

½ teaspoon baking powder

1 tablespoon All-Purpose Adobo (page 20)

1 teaspoon sazón (see page 19)

1½ cups water

Canola oil for frying

Bring a large pot of salted water to boil over medium-high heat. Place the potatoes in the water and cook for 10 to 15 minutes, or until they are fork-tender. Set aside to cool completely. When the potatoes are cool, cut them in half. Fold a slice of ham and a slice of cheese into squares and lay them between the pieces of a potato, creating a sandwich. Secure in place with two toothpicks. Repeat with the remaining potatoes, ham, and cheese. Set aside.

In a mixing bowl, combine the flour, baking powder, adobo, sazón, and water, stirring until you have a thick batter.

Line a baking sheet with paper towels and set near the stove. Fill a 2-quart pot with 4 inches of canola oil and place over medium-high heat. You want enough oil to submerge the guichis. Heat the oil until it registers 350°F on an instant-read thermometer. (Sprinkle in a little flour; if the oil sizzles, it's ready for frying.)

Submerge a potato sandwich into the batter, then place in the hot oil and fry for 3 to 6 minutes on one side. Flip it and fry for 3 to 6 minutes more, or until golden brown. Remember, the potato itself is already cooked—it's just a matter of getting the right texture of the batter. Using tongs, transfer the guichi to the prepared baking sheet. Repeat until the remaining guichis are fried.

Remove the toothpicks from the guichis and serve immediately.

Arepas de Coco

Makes 12 (4-inch) arepas

Yaniclecas, yani-clecas, and yaniqueque are all Dominican bastardizations of johnnycakes. From the Dominican Republic, these fritters made of flour found their way to Puerto Rico, where they're sometimes known as domplines, and more popularly as arepas. They are crispy, fried, and airy, and if you cook them right, they'll puff up enough so you can slit them in half and stuff them with delicious fillings. Sometimes the filling is just placed on top, and it can consist of pulled pork, churrasco (skirt steak), chicken, fried pork chunks, or a seafood salad.

2 cups all-purpose flour

2 tablespoons granulated sugar

½ teaspoon kosher salt

1½ teaspoons baking powder

1 cup coconut milk

Canola oil for frying

Ensalada de Pulpo y Camarones (page 90) for serving

In a large mixing bowl, combine the flour, sugar, salt, and baking powder, mixing with your hands. Add the coconut milk, switch to a plastic bench scraper, and mix with scooping motions until a shaggy dough forms.

Flour a work surface, turn the dough onto it, and knead until the dough forms a smooth ball; it will be soft and sticky. Using the scraper or your hands, place the dough in another bowl, cover, and set aside for 20 to 30 minutes.

Re-flour the work surface, then turn the dough onto it. Using a rolling pin, roll out the dough until it's ⅛ inch thick. Using a 4-inch round cookie cutter, biscuit cutter, or the mouth of a cup or glass, cut out as many circles as you can. Gather up the dough scraps, reroll, and cut out another batch of circles.

Place a wire cooling rack in a baking sheet and set near the stove. Fill a 10-inch cast-iron skillet with ½ inch of canola oil and place over medium-high heat. You want enough oil to cover the arepas. Heat the oil until it registers 350°F on an instant-read thermometer. (Add a tiny piece of dough; if it starts to sizzle but doesn't disintegrate, the oil is ready.)

Place a few dough circles at a time into the hot oil and fry for 30 seconds to 1 minute, or until deep golden brown. Using tongs or a slotted spoon, flip the circles and fry for 30 seconds to 1 minute more; they should puff up. Transfer the circles to the prepared rack and repeat to fry the remaining dough.

Serve the arepas, hot, with ensalada de pulpo.

Barriguitas de Vieja

Makes 20 barriguitas

The smell of autumn seems to appear overnight when you least expect it. You wake up one morning to a chill and the aroma of loamy earth, you pull an oversize blanket from the closet's clutches, and put it in its rightful place upon your bed. The air's arctic tinge starts to seep through your windows when you let the soft pink light in.

In my hometown of Sacramento, sandhill cranes click from above, their migratory path cutting right through my childhood ghetto. We neighborhood kids would lounge in the beds of abandoned trucks and stare up for hours, a moment to escape our forsaken community and its blight by watching the V-formation of the elegant long-necked birds. The evening's golden hour generated goldenrod rays onto Tudor homes, casting their bricks deep-red. At night, the glowing light from houses spilled out of picture windows onto damp sidewalks, taunting me. Acorns and dried leaves crunched underfoot as the wind wove through the leaves, clapping a jubilant physitheism as it sent off their foliage kin like confetti.

My nana's pumpkin fritters are a favorite autumnal treat. I suspect she didn't pay much attention to what varieties were ideal for certain cooking applications because the day after Halloween, she'd take my jack-o'-lantern and turn it into fritters. A pumpkin was a pumpkin. I wouldn't always carve my pumpkin but, would rather draw on it, leaving the guts intact. I had (have) a tendency to anthropomorphize everything, and I always felt bad for the pumpkin, but just drawing on Jack didn't protect him from Nana. His toothless, menacing grin rapidly disappeared with every butcher knife hack. As I squealed and pleaded, Nana half-shouted back, "You wanna eat fritters?!"

She'd remove all the pepitas and set them aside to dry them out so we could munch on them later. Then she'd combine Jack's guts with cinnamon, sugar, salt, flour, and vanilla. Soon you heard a splatter when the pumpkin dough hit the oil, the edges starting to samba as one side formed its crispiness. My excitement overshadowed my horror and couldn't be contained. The seconds seemed like hours to a child. Finally, Nana lifted the fritters out of the oil and placed them on a paper towel, sprinkled some iodized Morton's on top, and said, "Come, Gorda, come. Eat, Gorda, eat."

The fritters are weighty but eat light. Your teeth sink into the starchy soft center encased in a crispy shell, and their perfumed aroma wafts into your nose. They're sweet and savory, and their sprinkling of salt only seems to heighten those flavors. Traditionally, these fritters are called barriguitas de vieja, "old lady bellies," after the traditional method of deep-frying these wrinkly little mounds until the middle sinks in slightly to form a belly button. That divot never appeared in Nana's fritters because she never used enough oil to deep-fry them. Her fritters were always flat—thus her name for them: frituras de calabaza.

$\frac{1}{2}$-pound kabocha squash

$\frac{1}{2}$-pound sugar pumpkin

$\frac{1}{2}$ cup all-purpose flour

1 egg, beaten

1 teaspoon vanilla extract

2 tablespoons light brown sugar

1 tablespoon pumpkin pie spice

$\frac{1}{4}$ teaspoon baking powder

Canola oil for frying

Kosher salt

Preheat the oven to 400°F. Line a baking sheet with aluminum foil.

Cut the kabocha and pumpkin into wedges, leaving the skin intact, and place on the prepared baking sheet. Transfer to the oven and roast for 50 to 60 minutes, or until super-soft. Set aside to cool.

Peel away the skin of the kabocha and pumpkin and scoop the flesh into a large mixing bowl. Using a spatula, mash until relatively smooth. Add the flour and mix until just combined. Add the egg, vanilla, brown sugar, pumpkin pie spice, and baking powder and mix until well combined.

Place a wire cooling rack in a baking sheet and set near the stove. Fill a 10-inch cast-iron skillet with $\frac{1}{2}$ inch of canola oil and place over medium heat. You want enough oil to cover the barriguitas. Heat the oil until it registers 350°F on an instant-read thermometer. (Add a little bit of the pumpkin mixture; if the oil sizzles, it's ready for frying.)

Scoop a heaping 1 tablespoon of the pumpkin mixture into the oil and fry for 2 to 3 minutes. Using tongs or a slotted spoon, flip the barriguitas and fry for 2 to 3 minutes more, or until they are firm enough to pick up. The interior should still be slightly custardy and the exterior firm. Transfer the barriguitas to the prepared rack. Repeat with the remaining pumpkin mixture.

Sprinkle the barriguitas with salt and serve immediately.

Beans, Soups, and Stews

The year 2019 was the eye of an exaggerated and tasteless Instagrammable food storm. Mounds of millennial-pink scoops of cookie dough stacked on top of one another like gridlock traffic were created and ordered solely for the 'gram. But then, as the pandemic ripped through people's lives and inevitably sent them into their kitchens, we started to see a return to the simple and soulful replenishing foods of our past. Our feeds started to fill with sourdough breads, platters of roasted chicken, cups of consommé, and bowls of rice and beans. (If people could even find rice or beans during the beginning of quarantine.) Much like people believe chicken soup has magical healing powers (it does), I believe the same can be said about a pot of simple homemade beans.

Dolores Zavala is my godmother. Everyone calls her DeeDee. Nina DeeDee was born and raised in Stockton, California, but ended up in Sacramento after getting married. It's a long and traumatic story—and it ain't mine to tell—but Grandma and Nina DeeDee were acquainted first. Nina DeeDee started spending a lot of time at Nana's house, and eventually Nina DeeDee and my mother became good friends; this was in Sacramento during the 1960s. Nearly fifty years later, they're still comadres. Nina DeeDee has been back in Stockton for decades, and we regularly make the forty-five–minute drive to visit her.

The California Central Valley is where vineyards dating back to the 1880s wrap around towering viejo nopales. Ancient wooden utility poles still stand with their original Hemingray glass insulators, shining like precious jewels in the setting sun during the golden hour. Everything seems to be in tintype sepia tones of forgotten ancestors, whose things line the local thrift stores. It isn't until late summer and early fall that someone from the Central Valley remembers what color is, reminded by mini-trucks pulling small trailers filled with pumpkins from independent farmers. Bins filled with grapes and flatbeds stacked with bales of hay start to cross our path on highways. Stray blades of dried grass escape and flutter in the wind, leaving a wake of gold confetti for ho-hum drivers to pass through. Trucks filled to the brim with tomatoes may take a turn too sharply, leaving aisles of Roma globes and red splotches on the shoulders of off-ramps and byways. Take it all in. This part of California might be the last of the Steinbeckian prototype—the San Joaquin Valley, where ghostly ancestors lurk under mighty native *Quercus*, the oaks that dot the landscape. These foothills lead to gold-miner territory, where nuggets of gems can still be found and many a man lost his fortune and his mind. Summer is golden rolling hills with windmills. The coast where whales play in the waves alongside king salmon. And near the center of it all is Sacramento. Where I was born.

When I walk into Nina's 1920's bungalow in unincorporated Stockton, it feels like the type of house where you want to wake up on Christmas morning and smells like the most comfortable used bookstore. There's an old potbelly wood-burning stove that sits in the corner of the living room; its spout can be seen from the outside at the end of the gravel driveway if you stand next to the almond tree. It billows out thick plumes of smoke that drift over the barbwire fence and into the ditches that line the road with no sidewalks. I know Nina DeeDee is in her seventies, but she has no wrinkles. Her skin is as smooth as the inside of the shed bark of an American sycamore. She stopped dying her hair, and now it is various shades of white, with silver in her windswept bangs. She and my mother affectionately talk shit to each other in a way that people don't allow these days. I feel bad for those people because real intimacy and honesty are two essential qualities in genuine friendships.

Nina DeeDee is the last of the unconditional lovers. She's a part of Stockton's Chicano history; a romanticized and idealistic time that will never exist again. It's in the way she talks, the way she cooks, and the way she chooses her partners. It's also in the way she unquestionably allowed me to collapse into her arms and weep after my nana passed away. When I take a seat on one of her overstuffed couches in the dark living room, I have a partial view of the kitchen. Its golden light spills in, and there's a sliver of a view of Nina DeeDee standing at the stove. It feels like I'm peeping through a keyhole. She's starting her beans. She makes beans at least once a week. She maniacally straggles through her patinaed kitchen, the floor groaning under her feet, the gas range heating up the entire room. She fusses and curses everyone. Her voice is raspy with a tinge of Chicana cadence bouncing off her Bauer bowls and pouring out of the doorway. She fills her pot with tap water. The beans that are soaked overnight follow. She roughly slices white onions and garlic. Into the pot they go. The galley kitchen won't hold more than one cook at a time, and yet we seem to take our turns impatiently passing the cauldron of bubbling beans. They'll bubble away for hours, just the right amount of time for a visit, a coffee, a game of dominoes, and possibly an unplanned nap.

Later, she makes sopa de arroz, which, despite its name, is not a soup but rather what you might know as Spanish rice: a dry rice mixture simmered in chicken broth, onions, garlic, and tomato sauce. Then it's time to make tortillas. While she's mixing together flour, warm water, and scant baking powder, then forming a dough, I ask her where she learned to make tortillas. Her reply? "My tia had a cantina down in Guadalajara." (It's the first time I've heard this story.) She places a clear Pyrex bowl over the dough and leaves it to rest. When she returns, she pinches off a piece and cradles it in the meaty L-section between her thumb and index finger. She then places it on her Formica counter, rolls it out until thin, and lays it on the comal. The smell of char swells in the kitchen, and the dough starts to form a single bubble, informing us it's time to flip. She places the hot tortilla in a kitchen towel, covers it, and repeats the process. She stirs the beans and adds a heaping mound of her secret ingredients: Monterey Jack cheese and a little milk. The mound of milky-white shredded cheese starts to melt and ooze into the bean water, creating elastic strands that adhere to her mixing spoon. The broth has turned thick.

When guests line up in the warm kitchen, the frenzy of gathering and passing plates and utensils begins. We serve ourselves from the steaming pots of beans and rice on the stove, grabbing a few tortillas. We sit down at the aged dining room table and silently dig into our homemade tortillas, beans, and rice. Home. Made. The beans are simple, only five ingredients. And yet they are buttery, creamy, salty, and floral. They are meaty and melty. We're all thinking, *This is the single best thing I've eaten in a long time.* My nina apologizes for not having company-appropriate food in the house. She complains that the tortillas are tough (they're not), and the beans are too simple (they're not). And my mom finally tells her, "Oh, will you just shut up and eat?!" And that makes me feel warm and fuzzy inside.

Toward the end of my grandmother's life, after a few bypass surgeries, the doctors banned her from eating so many of the things she enjoyed. Ham hocks were prohibited. The acidity of tomato sauce would give her heartburn. She lost interest in eating most things. But she never turned down a simple bowl of rice and beans. Rice and beans were life. It didn't matter if they were pinto, pink, or red. We had to start making beans in the way of Nina DeeDee. And so, Nina DeeDee's beans became Nana's beans.

Nina DeeDee's Beans

Makes 8 to 10 servings

You can use any type of bean for this recipe. My family most commonly uses pinto, peruano, yellow eye, and kidney. In the morning, I like to cook some Mexican chorizo in a cast-iron skillet, mix in leftover beans and some of the cooking liquid, and then mash them all together. Serve with fried eggs and hot flour tortillas.

1 pound dried beans (see recipe introduction)

1 large white or yellow onion

8 garlic cloves

2 cups grated Monterey Jack cheese or queso Oaxaca

Kosher salt

Spread out the beans on a baking sheet and pick out any rocks and impurities. Place the beans in a large pot and add water to cover by 3 inches. Cut the onion in half through its equator, remove the skin but keep the core (root) intact, and add to the pot. Smash the garlic with a knife, remove and discard the skins, and add to the pot.

Place the pot over high heat and bring to a boil for 5 to 10 minutes, then turn the heat to low and let simmer, uncovered, for 2 to 4 hours (see Note). Check the beans and stir them every 30 minutes, adding more water to cover as needed. The pot should always have 2 to 3 inches of liquid in it so the beans don't burn. When the beans are cooked to your liking, stir in the cheese.

Season the beans with salt before serving.

Note: How long the beans cook depends entirely on your doneness preference (al dente versus creamy) and on the brand of beans. If you're using a premium brand of dried beans, like Rancho Gordo, the beans tend to be fresher and won't take as long to cook. But, if you're using supermarket beans that may have been there for a while, they'll take much longer to get tender. Occasionally, I add a ham hock to the beans with the water. If the ham hock is of good quality, it'll take 3 to 4 hours for it and the beans to become tender.

Puerto Rican Habichuelas

Makes 4 to 6 servings

Many people use canned beans for a shortcut. I rarely do, but I'm not against it. If you decide to use canned beans, warm them and their liquid in a pot to start.

1 pound dried pinto, peruano, yellow eye, or kidney beans, or 1 (15-ounce) can pinto or kidney beans

Achiote oil (see page 19) for sautéing

1 large white or yellow onion, coarsely diced

8 garlic cloves, coarsely diced

1 large russet potato, peeled and cut into medium dice

1 to 2 cups sofrito (see page 23)

1 cup tomato sauce

1 tablespoon sazón (see page 19)

2 dried bay leaves

Kosher salt

Freshly ground black pepper

1 cup water

Spread out the beans on a baking sheet and pick out any rocks and impurities. Place the beans in a large pot and add water to cover by 3 inches.

Place the pot over high heat and bring to a boil for 5 to 10 minutes, then turn the heat to low and let simmer, uncovered, for 2 to 4 hours (see Note, page 63). Check the beans and stir them every 30 minutes, adding more water to cover as needed. The pot should always have 2 to 3 inches of liquid in it so the beans don't burn.

In a separate large pot, combine the achiote oil and onion, place over medium heat, and sauté for 2 to 4 minutes, or until translucent. Add the garlic and sauté for 1 to 2 minutes more. Add the potato and continue to sauté for 5 to 7 minutes. Then add the sofrito, tomato sauce, sazón, bay leaves; season with salt and pepper; and mix to combine. Add the beans and their cooking liquid and 1 cup water, then cover and cook for 15 to 20 minutes, until the potato has softened.

Ladle the beans into bowls and serve immediately.

Mami's Chicken Soup with Bisquick Dumplings

Makes 4 to 6 servings

As with several of Mami's recipes, this one includes a semi-homemade trend. When I would get sick as a kid, Mami would force her brujeria remedies onto me: Lipton tea bags steeped with a knob of ginger; 7UP; plenty of water topped with a splash of juice; and chicken soup—a simple composition containing no more than six main ingredients. And, since she wasn't making two different meals, she'd top it off with dumplings for substance so *she'd* feel full. When my throat starts to get scratchy and my body aches, I will quickly make this soup, sometimes adding fresh ginger and leaving out the dumplings. When I'm sad, I will quickly make this soup, always adding the dumplings. It cures sickness and sadness. To this day, I don't like to consume soups that have a lot of ingredients. Keep it simple, stupid.

3 tablespoons olive oil

1 medium yellow onion, coarsely diced

2 celery stalks, coarsely chopped

6 garlic cloves, minced

5 bone-in, skin-on chicken thighs

1 chicken bouillon cube

4 carrots, peeled and coarsely chopped

2 large russet potatoes, cut into large dice

Kosher salt

Freshly ground black pepper

Dumplings

2¼ cups Bisquick Original Pancake and Baking Mix

⅔ cup milk

Add 2 tablespoons of the olive oil to a large pot and place over medium-high heat. Add the onion and celery and sauté for 2 to 3 minutes, occasionally shifting the veg around. Add the garlic and sauté for 1 minute more. Continue to shift the veg around to keep it from browning too much. Transfer the onion mixture to a bowl and set aside.

In the same pot, without wiping it out, over medium-high heat, warm the remaining 1 tablespoon olive oil. Add the chicken thighs skin-side down and brown for 1 to 2 minutes. Flip the chicken, return the onion mixture to the pot, and then add the bouillon cube, two of the carrots, and enough water to just cover the chicken. Bring to a simmer, cover, and cook for 1 hour.

Remove the chicken from the pot, place it on a cutting board, and hack it into pieces. This is the time to remove the bone and skin if you want; I like to keep them. Add the chicken, potatoes, and remaining two carrots to the pot and cook for 15 to 25 minutes more, or until the potatoes and additional carrots are tender. Season with salt and pepper.

To make the dumplings: Place the baking mix in a bowl and stir in the milk just until incorporated. Drop the biscuit dough a heaping tablespoon at a time into the simmering soup and cook for 8 to 10 minutes, or until the dough is firm and puffy.

Serve the soup and dumplings immediately.

A Chicken Curry

Makes 4 to 6 servings

Although this dish has no connection to a true Indian curry, it is something that I do make frequently. It's quick, full of flavor, and flexes sofrito's versatility and convenience. Sofrito can be made ahead and frozen, and it crosses cultural barriers. You can use a variety of fresh and in-season vegetables—like zucchini and green beans—or you could also use frozen or canned lima beans. I've done all the above. A true Diasporican recipe.

2 tablespoons olive oil

1 medium yellow onion, coarsely chopped

6 garlic cloves, smashed and coarsely minced

3 tablespoons curry spice blend

3 tablespoons garam masala

2 tablespoons Illyanna's Adobo (page 20)

½ cup sofrito (see page 23)

2 cups water, or as needed

6 bone-in, skin-on chicken thighs

1-pound kabocha squash, skin left on, cut into 2-inch chunks

1 (15-ounce) can coconut milk

Kosher salt

Freshly ground black pepper

Add the olive oil to a large pot and place over medium heat. When the oil is shimmering, add the onion and sauté for 1 to 2 minutes. Add the garlic and sauté for 1 minute more, or until translucent. Add the curry spice blend, garam masala, and adobo and let them bloom, about 30 seconds, while continuously stirring. Add the sofrito and cook for a few seconds, continuing to stir, then add the water and chicken. Turn the heat to medium-high and bring to a boil. Immediately turn the heat to low, cover, and let simmer for 30 minutes.

Add the kabocha, coconut milk, and more water to cover, if needed, to the pot and bring back to a low simmer. Cover and let cook for 10 to 20 minutes, or until the kabocha is tender when pierced with a knife. Season with salt and pepper.

Serve the curry immediately.

Rabbit Fricassee with Chayote

Makes 4 servings

I remember the first time that I ate rabbit. Like many of my memories of Nana, I was sitting at the kitchen table, facing her back as she cooked. She was frying meat and the smell was alluring. When she placed the plate of bone-in meat in front of me, I picked up a steaming-hot little lollipop-looking drumette and nibbled in delight. It was the most intense and concentrated meat flavor I had ever tasted. "This is the best fried chicken, Nana!" I exclaimed. "That's not chicken, that's rabbit," she replied. Little Me paused, took a look at the niblet, and began to cry. And then I continued to cry-eat. Coincidentally, it was just around the time that my pet rabbit, Rainbow, went missing. I'm not saying we were eating Rainbow. I'm just saying. . . .

2 tablespoons olive oil

1 small yellow onion, coarsely chopped

6 garlic cloves, smashed and coarsely minced

1 (2½- to 3-pound) rabbit, cut into pieces

Kosher salt

Freshly ground black pepper

1 cup sofrito (see page 23)

2 dried bay leaves

¼ cup dry white wine

1 tablespoon soy sauce

1 to 2 cups water, or as needed

2 chayote, cut into irregular 2-inch chunks

2 large russet potatoes, cut into irregular 2-inch chunks

Add the olive oil to a large pot and place over medium heat. When the oil is shimmering, add the onion and sauté 1 to 2 minutes. Add the garlic and sauté 1 minute more, or until translucent. Place the rabbit pieces in the pot and shift them around with a rubber spatula to brown, 3 to 7 minutes. Season with salt and pepper.

Add the sofrito to the rabbit and cook for a few seconds, continuing to shift everything in the pot around. Add the bay leaves and wine and cook until most of the wine steam has stopped. Stir in the soy sauce and enough of the water to cover. Turn the heat to medium-high, cover, and bring to a boil. Immediately turn the heat to low, cover, and let simmer, stirring occasionally, for 30 minutes.

Add the chayote, potatoes, and more water to cover, if needed, to the pot and bring back to a simmer. Cover and let cook for 10 to 20 minutes, or until the meat is tender and the chayote is still on the firmer side. (It should be the consistency of zucchini that you prefer; I like my zucchini on the firm side.) The sauce should have thickened from the starch released from the potatoes. If it didn't thicken enough for your liking, spoon a few of the potato chunks into a bowl, mash, and add back to the broth. Remove the bay leaves.

Serve the fricassee immediately.

Sancocho

Makes 10 servings

It's going to be impossible for some of you to find all the tubers—ñame, yellow batata dulce, malanga, yautía—that normally go into this soup-stew, which is traditionally chock-full of filling, starchy vegetables. The good news is that there are available varieties of the same tubers or similar vegetables at your local Asian markets. (I've used purple sweet potatoes that I found at the farmers' market, for example.) This stew is unfairly easy to make for the amount of flavor you get from it. Serving with rice is optional but also very Puerto Rican.

2 tablespoons garlic powder

2 tablespoons onion powder

1 tablespoon ground cumin

2 tablespoons sazón (see page 19)

1½ pounds boneless beef chuck roast, cut into 1-inch cubes

3 tablespoons olive oil

1 large yellow onion, coarsely chopped

4 garlic cloves, coarsely chopped

½ cup sofrito (see page 23)

2 cups water, or as needed

1 cup beef broth

1 tablespoon soy sauce

1 tablespoon fish sauce

1 plátano, peeled (see page 12) and cut into ½-inch-thick slices

1 small yuca, peeled and cut into 1-inch pieces

1 small yautía or large russet potato, peeled and cut into 1-inch pieces

1 small kabocha squash, skin left on and cut into 1-inch pieces

1 ear corn, cut into 2-inch-thick medallions

Kosher salt

Freshly ground black pepper

In a small bowl, combine the garlic powder, onion powder, cumin, and sazón. Sprinkle this seasoning mixture over the beef, ensuring the meat is well coated. Set aside.

In a large wide pot over medium heat, combine 1 tablespoon of the olive oil and the onion and sauté for 2 to 3 minutes, or until soft. Add the garlic and sauté for 1 minute more, or until translucent. Transfer the onion and garlic mixture to a bowl and set aside.

Place the pot, without wiping it out, over medium-high heat and add the remaining 2 tablespoons olive oil. When the oil is shimmering, add the beef and sear the cubes on all sides, 6 to 8 minutes. Return the onion mixture to the pot and stir to incorporate. Add the sofrito and stir in the water, beef broth, soy sauce, and fish sauce. Turn the heat to low, cover, and let simmer for 2 hours, or until the meat is tender.

Add the plátano and yuca to the pot, cover with more water if necessary, and cook for 10 to 20 minutes, or until tender. Add the yautía, kabocha, and corn and cook for 5 to 10 minutes more, or until tender. Season with salt and pepper.

Serve the sancocho immediately.

Pastele Stew

Makes 10 servings

Elisabeth Souza (Ross) opened the Pastele Shop in Honolulu in 1981. In 2018, Elisabeth passed away at the age of one hundred, and her daughters are now running the restaurant. Elisabeth, who was Chinese and Hawaiian, was born and raised on a sugarcane plantation, where the "camps" were segregated by ethnicity. Her Uncle Mahana married a woman from the Puerto Rican camp, Aunt Jenny, and Elisabeth learned how to make pasteles from her. Elisabeth would use this craft to provide for her family, selling pasteles in local bars and, eventually, opening the first pastele shop on the island of Oʻahu.

I knew there were Puerto Ricans living in Hawaiʻi. You come across information about that all the time when you're attempting to find your way down an internet rabbit hole at three o'clock in the morning. What I hadn't known was how their food had evolved through time, geography, and necessity. And I really didn't know how the food was still evolving (pastele lumpia or pastele sausage, anyone?) and that pasteles were so ingrained in Hawaiian culture that most don't even realize their Puerto Rican origin. What Da Borinkees (the name with which Puerto Ricans of Hawaiʻi identify themselves) dub *pastele stew*, Puerto Ricans of Puerto Rico call *pastel al caldero*. Boricuas use Spanish green olives, Da Borinkees use black olives. The Pastele Shop serves pastele stew over rice and topped with an egg, turning it into a loco moco. Don't forget to save some of the stew to encase in lumpia wrappers and fry the next day because, in Hawaiʻi, they draw on the Filipino foodways and make pastele lumpias.

½ cup achiote oil (see page 19)

2 pounds pork shoulder, or boneless pork country-style ribs, coarsely diced

Kosher salt

Freshly ground black pepper

2 tablespoons ground cumin

2 tablespoons dried oregano

2 cups water

1 cup tomato sauce

1 cup sofrito (see page 23)

Thai chiles, to taste

2 cups canned black olives

8 to 12 guineos, peeled (see page 12)

Basic White Rice (page 164) for serving

Add the achiote oil to a large pot and place over high heat. Add the pork; season with salt, pepper, cumin, and oregano; and brown on all sides, 5 to 6 minutes. Add the water, tomato sauce, sofrito, and chiles and turn the heat to low. Cover and braise for 1 hour, then add the olives.

Place a box grater in a large bowl. Using the side with the smallest holes (the ones that protrude outward and are spiky), grate the guineos; this will turn the guineos into a paste rather than strands. Add the guineos to the pot ½ cup at a time, waiting about 3 minutes to add the next ½ cup. By gradually dropping them in, you're forming dumpling-like masses. (You can add all the guineos at one time, but it will make the stew denser.) After all the guineos have been placed in the pot, let simmer, uncovered, for 45 minutes to 1 hour.

Ladle the stew over rice and serve immediately.

Caldo Santo

Makes 2 or 3 servings

Every year during Holy Week, the week leading up to Easter, there's a competition in Loíza—easily the cradle of African foodways in Puerto Rico—in which myriad members of the community gather to make caldo santo, a seafood chowder. In typical fashion, everyone has their own way of doing things, and their preferences of ingredients vary. However, the template remains similar: a coconut milk base, achiote for color, root vegetables, and seafood as protein. At the festival, aisles of people cook caldo santo, competing for bragging rights.

Some still create the broth in the traditional and laborious way—making the coconut milk from scratch. Using a grater, the white coconut flesh is shaved into a bowl, sometimes a little water is added, and then the coconut is squeezed. Squeezed. SQUEEZED. You better have strong hands for this step. Achiote goes into a pilón, and hot oil is poured over the seeds, coaxing out all their floral, musky redness. The seeds samba in effervescence. The achiote oil is poured into the caldo of alabaster coconut milk, and the entire broth immediately turns Creamsicle orange. Green plantains, calabaza, yautía, pana, and sofrito go into the pot. The seafood follows as the finishing touch. Some people include olives, corn, and sweet potato. Most use a combination of local blue land crabs, red snapper, and shrimp. Others throw in salmon.

I've got an objection to the fact that salmon seems to show up more and more on my visits to Puerto Rico. (Show me where the fuck you can catch a salmon in any of the island's rivers?) It's another one of those import/export trade-offs, except they export the island's cosmic mahi-mahi and spiny lobster in exchange for affordable and flavorless farmed salmon. No bueno.

But since my recipe for caldo santo is semi-endemic to Northern California, I do use my absolute favorite fish and shellfish, which is in-season wild California king salmon and local Dungeness crab. I might have also slipped in my favorite blended herb seasoning and a bouillon cube. These are personal and optional. It's different but the same.

continued ▶

Caldo Santo, continued

1 plátano, peeled (see page 12) and coarsely cut into large chunks

1 yuca, peeled and coarsely cut into large chunks

1 small kabocha squash, peeled and coarsely cut into large chunks

¼ cup achiote seeds

1 (15-ounce) can coconut milk

¼ cup sofrito (see page 23)

1 pound cleaned Dungeness crabmeat

8 ounces 16/20-count shrimp, peeled and deveined

1 tablespoon canola oil

1 pound salmon fillets

Kosher salt

Freshly ground black pepper

1 small lime or lemon, cut into wedges (optional)

1 small avocado, sliced (optional)

Set a colander over a stockpot. Bring a large pot of water to boil over high heat. Add the plátano, yuca, and kabocha to the water and boil for 5 to 8 minutes, or until they are fork-tender. Pour the contents of the pot into the colander, reserving the water that the vegetables were cooked in (now a broth). Set the vegetables aside and pour the broth back into the pot.

Turn the heat to medium and bring the broth to a simmer. Add the achiote seeds and let simmer for 2 to 4 minutes. Pour the achiote broth through a sieve into a bowl, removing all the seeds. Return the broth to the pot. Add the coconut milk and 2 tablespoons of the sofrito and bring to a simmer (but not a boil, the coconut milk might separate) for 5 to 10 minutes, or until the broth has reduced and thickened. Add the crab and shrimp to the pot and continue to simmer for 5 to 6 minutes. Turn off the heat and keep warm.

Add the canola oil to a large cast-iron skillet and place over medium heat. Add the salmon and sear for 8 to 10 minutes, depending on its thickness, or until cooked to your preferred doneness. Using a spatula, transfer the salmon to a plate and set aside.

Add the remaining 2 tablespoons sofrito and the cooked vegetables to the shellfish mixture, letting the vegetables simmer for 1 to 2 minutes, or until they are warmed through. Season with salt and pepper.

Spoon the caldo santo into shallow bowls and top each with a piece of cooked salmon. If desired, garnish with a squeeze of lime juice and a slice of avocado and serve immediately.

Seafood

People think of seafood when they think of the islands but are often disappointed when they go to Puerto Rico. I'm frequently asked, "Where's the fresh seafood?" The easiest answer that I can offer is they export most of it! Between pollution and the complex regulations governing local fishing, the island's own fishing industry could never truly develop.

Makeshift traps made from milk crates can be found in the waters that surround Puerto Rico's shorelines. They're illegal. And incredibly harmful to the environment. But sometimes that's the only way in which locals can procure fresh seafood from their ancestral waters. The politically strategic collapse of traditional agriculture meant the private and public sectors demanded coastal space for leisure-based pursuits instead of being used for food production. Coastal gentrification. Those sectors continue to threaten the existence of ancestral fishing communities throughout Puerto Rico, including the industrial pollution of lagoons and estuaries, leaving locals with minimal access to the shoreline to fish. In addition, anglers need a license and the only way to acquire such a permit is to visit one of the seven regional offices of the Department for Natural Resources. *Seven* offices. In all of Puerto Rico.

And there are fish to be caught in these waters. The reefs hold some of the more common offerings that you'll find at restaurants in Puerto Rico, including red snapper, which is known locally as chillo (sometimes spelled *chio*). Mahi-mahi and wahoo run rampant in the deep ocean just a few miles offshore. Mahi-mahi is a huge sort of Neanderthal-looking fish with beautiful chartreuse opalescence and turquoise coloring. Both mahi-mahi and wahoo come into this area at different times of the year, traveling on the Yucatán's warm ocean current that flows

Opposite page inset: Hans Haverman fileting, H&H Fresh Fish, Santa Cruz, California.

through the Caribbean from South America and the Gulf of Mexico. Unfortunately, the luxury of catching these fish seems to be restricted mostly to commercial fishermen and those who book charter trips—people with money or connections.

The oyster industry of Puerto Rico is virtually nonexistent. Marketing and commerce of locally produced oysters has changed little since the 1950s. Soon after the island was acquired by the United States, an abundance of small oysters was reported growing on the aerial roots of mangrove trees bordering the lagoons, and occasionally a few of those oysters were gathered and sent in the shell to the largest cities, where they were peddled through the streets. Today, fishermen in Boquerón gather some of the larger oysters by cutting them from the mangrove roots with their machetes. The United States government has spent years trying to find a way to commercialize the oyster industry in Puerto Rico. The island's small oysters are considered too tiny to be profitable, and at one time the powers that be considered introducing a foreign species of oysters, hoping it would give tourists larger ones to consume and therefore bigger profits for the administration. But it never worked out in the land of "mañana en la mañana." Although some vendors do sell oysters imported from the States, these tiny native oysters prevailed. Their diminutive size demands consumption in mighty portions. You can see un-iced stacks of these little mangrove oysters on vendors' carts all along the west coast of the island in Rincón, Boquerón, La Parguera, and other stops.

Now that every one of Puerto Rico's natural resources has been subsumed, including its fish and shellfish, the United States is biding its time to figure out what to do with Puerto Rico. Independence or statehood? You want to know what statehood would look like? A Disneyland version of Puerto Rico; just look at Hawai'i.

Shucking oysters, Rincón, Puerto Rico.

Puerto Rican coastline.

Hog Island Oyster Co., Marshall, California.

Grilled Oysters

Makes 12 oysters

The nearly extinct Olympia oysters of Northern California share some similarities with the oysters in Puerto Rico. They're small. And they're eaten without fuss. This recipe is simple and direct, introducing the combination of briny oysters and spicy, floral pique, which already has all the seasonings that you'd have to mince by hand to create a sauce. Mignonette, who?

Summer in San Francisco is cold and foggy. It's amusing to see tourists show up in their T-shirts and shorts only to be met by Karl the Fog's wet, misty droplets. If we're lucky enough to live near the coast, we're grilling oysters—fresh oysters harvested in Tomales Bay. That's where you'll find Hog Island Oysters. Opened in 1983, their 160 acres are located in some of the most isolated areas of Miwok territory. There's no cell connection out there. I never tire of sitting at one of their sun-bleached wooden tables, shucking and slurping a bushel of oysters with friends while the sun and coastal breeze wash across my face.

12 oysters

¼ cup pique (see page 23)

Prepare a hot charcoal grill or preheat a gas grill. (I prefer charcoal.)

Place the oysters on the grill grate, flat-side up. You want to make sure the convex (bumpy) side of the shells is resting on the grill grate. Close the grill lid and cook for 3 to 5 minutes.

When the oysters are ready, the shells will pop open and little spit bubbles will appear around the edges. Keep checking. The meat will sometimes be attached to the top shell. If it is, just release it with an oyster knife and slide it back into the bottom half of the shell with all the oyster liquor. Discard the top shells and place the oysters on a serving plate.

Drizzle the pique over the oysters while they're still hot so the sauce warms a little, and serve immediately.

Note: If you're grilling oysters, you don't have to do the hard work of shucking. The heat of the grill will do that for you. But, for some reason, if you've gotten it into your head that you must shuck . . . slide an oyster knife into the groove between the bottom and the top of the oyster near the hinge, giving the knife blade a little twist to help the oyster's top shell pop open.

Salmorejo

Makes 4 servings

Once, when I was being interviewed on an Instagram Live by another Puerto Rican content creator, I confessed that I didn't like olives. Judging by the pained twist of his eyebrows, I quickly offered the context that, while I don't like them, I still use them when I'm cooking Puerto Rican food. One, because it's what my grandma did. Two, because culinary school taught me to balance flavors, sometimes using olives or lemon juice to incorporate the brightness that heavy foods and tastes often need. Then again, that's what Puerto Rican cuisine already does by using vinegar and olives, so I went back to square one. Sometimes, I'll skip the olives in recipes and use just the brine. In this dish, I'll often sub fresh lemon and a splash of vinegar in place of the olives. I love lemon and fish together.

2 tablespoons olive oil

1 yellow onion, cut into small dice

1 red bell pepper, cut into small dice

4 garlic cloves, finely minced

½ cup sofrito (see page 23)

1 teaspoon sazón (see page 19)

1 teaspoon All-Purpose Adobo
(page 20)

¼ cup Manzanilla olives, chopped,
or a splash of olive brine

1 pound Dungeness lump crabmeat
(see Note)

Kosher salt

Freshly ground white pepper

Basic White Rice (page 164)
for serving

Add the olive oil to a skillet and place over medium-high heat. Add the onion and bell pepper and sauté for 2 to 4 minutes, or until translucent. Add the garlic and sauté for 1 to 2 minutes more, then stir in the sofrito, sazón, and adobo. Add the olives (or, if you're like me, the brine), dump in the crab, and mix gently to combine well. Cook for 5 to 10 minutes, season with salt and white pepper, and cook for 5 to 10 minutes more.

Serve the salmorejo over rice.

Note: During Dungeness season, fish mongers and supermarkets sell containers of cooked, cleaned, and shelled lump crabmeat. It's literally a container of just the meat.

Califas Shrimp

Makes 4 servings

The first time I made this recipe was for a cooking demonstration at the San Francisco Ferry Plaza Farmers Market. I used shrimp from one of the regular vendors, H&H Fresh Fish. I immediately became obsessed with their product—they have some of the most beautiful seafood I've encountered. Since 2003, Hans Haverman and Heidi Rhodes have been the resident seafood buyers at Santa Cruz Harbor, where H&H is based. They run a small and efficient operation that provides Bay Area residents with sustainable, regional seafood.

Puerto Rico has always been an island where the regional cooking depends entirely on available local resources. Colonization didn't change that. Then it was about local resources and the types of crops that haciendas grew, prices of imported foodstuffs, and international political climate. This is why Califas Shrimp is and is not a traditional Puerto Rican dish. It's one that eats like shrimp and grits, but combining seafood and funche has been a thing since enslaved Africans were forced to work in the sugarcane fields. Historically, bacalao was simmered with onions and tomatoes and served over funche. This cornmeal mush was cheaper than rice, which was a monetarily valuable commodity, and the mush was already something that enslaved people were used to eating. Slavers could appear to be doing a favor for enslaved people by forcing them to eat something relatively familiar when really it was just a cost-saving move to provide a nutrient-rich dish that could sustain a hard-working person for very little money.

¼ cup Mexican chorizo

½ cup orange juice

2 tablespoons lemon juice, plus ½ lemon

1 tablespoon sazón (see page 19)

½ teaspoon sambal (such as sambal oelek)

¼ cup sofrito (see page 23)

1 cup water

Kosher salt

Freshly ground black pepper

2 tablespoons salted butter

1 pound 26/30-count shrimp, peeled and deveined

Funche (page 174) for serving

Place a skillet over medium-high heat. Add the chorizo and sauté for about 4 minutes, or until the meat begins to brown and renders some fat. Stir in the orange juice, lemon juice, sazón, sambal, sofrito, and water to loosen the mixture. Season with salt and pepper. Scrape the chorizo and sauce into a bowl and set aside.

In the same pan, combine the butter and shrimp, season with salt and pepper, and cook for 1 minute. Using tongs, flip the shrimp and cook for 1 minute more; the shrimp should be slightly pink. Add the chorizo mixture and sauce and finish with a squeeze of lemon juice.

Spoon the funche into serving bowls, top with the shrimp-chorizo mixture, and serve immediately.

Empanadas de Scallops

Makes 18 to 20 empanadas

There are a few opportunities to show people that Puerto Rican cuisine can be regional. And empanadas de cetí is definitely one of them. Cetí, universally known as whitebait, are the immature baby fish of the at-risk sirajo goby—and other fish species—that swim upstream in the Río Grande de Arecibo. This seasonal run attracts cetí harvesters through the months of June to December. They stand at the base of the Arecibo River, where it meets the Atlantic Ocean, and capture the tiny fishes as they flow directly into fishing nets, mesh bags, or recycled burlap coffee sacks. The fishermen put the near-translucent fish into buckets of water for later use in dishes of cultural importance, such as empanadas, pastelillos, and arepas. If you're the squeamish type who doesn't want to get into the water with thousands of tiny fish, you can just purchase a bag of them at a roadside stand or bait shop. Or you can just consume prepared empanadas de cetí at one of the many coastal eateries in Arecibo. Cetí can be challenging for many people to find, so in my version of these empanadas, I decided to switch it up and use scallops.

When making achiote oil with manteca, you will need to cut the recipe in half and make it twice because the lard solidifies as it sits, and these empanadas take some time to assemble. So, you'll make one-half batch of the oil to fold into the masa as you're preparing it and then another half-batch when you're ready to assemble the empanadas.

12 guineos, peeled (see page 12)

1 incredibly firm plátano, peeled (see page 12)

1 small yautía blanca (also labeled white malanga), peeled

Kosher salt

¼ cup sofrito (see page 23)

2 cups achiote oil (see page 19), made with manteca, one-half recipe at a time

2 pounds scallops, coarsely chopped

Preheat the oven to 350°F.

Place a box grater in a large bowl. Using the side with the smallest holes (the ones that protrude outward and are spiky), grate the guineos, plátano, and yautía. Season with salt, add the sofrito, and stir to combine well. This is your empanada masa.

With a spoon, make a well in the middle of the masa. Pour ½ cup of the achiote oil through a sieve and directly but gradually into the well. Using the same spoon, quickly and carefully fold the oil into the masa. Add another ¼ cup achiote oil, again straining it through the sieve and folding it into the masa. Keep folding until all the oil has been absorbed and the masa has turned from Silly Putty brown to reddish orange.

Cut eighteen to twenty banana leaves, or parchment paper or aluminum foil, into 10-inch squares. Spoon 1 tablespoon of achiote oil on each square. Using the back of the spoon, spread the oil toward the edges of the square. Scoop 1 cup of the masa onto the achiote oil and form into a log in the middle of the square. Embed the scallop pieces in the masa. Starting with one side of the square, roll it over the dough log, encasing it and continuing to roll until the log is completely enclosed. You should have a cylindrical parcel. If the masa is peeking out of the sides, that's okay. Place the empanada on a baking sheet and repeat to form the remaining empanadas. Roast in the oven for 15 to 20 minutes.

Place the empanadas on individual plates, carefully cut open, and eat from the wrapping.

Note: There is only one difference between pasteles and empanadas—pasteles are boiled or steamed, while empanadas are roasted.

Dungeness Guanimes

Makes 2 or 3 servings

Guanimes are little dumplings that are traditionally steamed in plantain leaves. Some people use a mix of cornmeal and all-purpose flour. Some people use only flour. Some people use water instead of coconut milk. But, like for my funche (see page 174), I wanted to add more flavor to these. I find the all-flour dumplings on the heavier side; but in lean times, you use what you've got. They're served on the side or under a copious amount of acidic tomato sauce laced with bits of salted bacalao. Sometimes I find that the bacalao stew adds heaviness to a light dumpling and I want to change things up. A tiny bit. Out there somewhere, a Puerto Rican is cursing the very thought of my changing this dish. But since guanimes are usually made with bacalao anyway, and I'm using the West Coast's beloved Dungeness crab. . . .

Guanimes

1 cup coconut milk

1 cup water

1 tablespoon granulated sugar

Kosher salt

1½ cups yellow cornmeal

2 tablespoons olive oil

1 small yellow onion, coarsely diced

5 garlic cloves, coarsely minced

2 tablespoons All-Purpose Adobo (page 20)

1 (15-ounce) can coconut milk

2 teaspoons fish sauce

1 teaspoon ground achiote

1 pound Dungeness lump crabmeat (see Note, page 79)

8 ounces 16/20-count shrimp, peeled, deveined, and coarsely chopped

Lemon wedges for squeezing

To make the guanimes: In a small pot over medium heat, combine the coconut milk, water, and sugar; season with salt; stir to incorporate; and bring to a low simmer. Add the cornmeal and continue to stir vigorously until the dough comes together and looks thick and supple. Turn off the heat and set aside.

Cut twelve banana leaves, or parchment paper or aluminum foil, into 6-inch squares. Spoon about ⅓ cup of the dough onto a square and form into a log in the middle of the square, leaving a 2- to 3-inch border. Starting with one side of the square, roll it over the dough log, encasing it and continuing to roll until the log is completely enclosed. You should have a cylindrical parcel. Tie both ends with butcher's twine. (If you can't visualize this, Google "British Christmas Cracker." That's what the damn thing should look like.) Repeat to make the remaining parcels.

Bring a pot of water to a rolling boil over high heat. Add the parcels and boil for 8 to 10 minutes, or until firm. Turn off the heat and then dump out the water, leaving the guanimes in the pot with the lid on until you're ready to serve.

Add the olive oil to a skillet and place over medium-high heat. Add the onion and sauté for 2 to 3 minutes, or until translucent. Add the garlic and cook for 1 minute more, then stir in the adobo, coconut milk, and fish sauce. Add the achiote, turn the heat to low, and let barely simmer for 10 to 15 minutes. Stir in the crab and shrimp, cover the pot, and cook for 2 to 5 minutes, or until the shrimp are pink.

Cut the ends off the parcels, unroll the guanimes onto serving plates, and pour the crab-shrimp mixture over the tops. Garnish with a squeeze of lemon juice and serve immediately.

Bacalao Ensalada

Makes 2 or 3 servings

It's common for people to flip their lids with this salad, adding hard-boiled eggs, raw bell peppers, alcaparrado, tomatoes, avocados, and more. Mami and Nana never ate it this way. Instead, they chose to go the route where the few ingredients shined; they prioritized clean flavors. This is one of the Puerto Rican dishes that I remember my mother making together with Nana. It's one of Mami's favorite dishes, and I never saw her make it for just herself. And I never saw Nana make it for anyone else. Thinly slicing white onions in Nana's teensy-weensy kitchen, they'd cook butt to gut as if no remorse or resentment existed between them. I'd watch the two of them, barely saying a word to each other, both of their brown foreheads furrowed, never looking directly at each other. And then they'd sit down, eating in almost silence. And yet, I think this is one of the few times that Mami ever felt totally nurtured by Nana. It was their dish and no one else's. Serve it like they did, with viandas (see page 186).

10 (16-ounce) bacalao fillets

1 small white onion, cut into extremely thin slices

$\frac{1}{3}$ cup olive oil (preferably a mild-flavored one, such as Star brand)

$\frac{1}{2}$ lemon

Kosher salt

Freshly ground black pepper

Put the bacalao in a large pot of cold water. Place over low heat, bring to a simmer, and cook—keeping an eye on it at all times because it will boil over—for 15 to 30 minutes, or until the fish starts to flake apart on its own. Taste for saltiness; if it's too salty for you, drain the water, add new water, and simmer again for 15 minutes more.

Using tongs or a fine-mesh strainer, remove the bacalao from the water and transfer to a cutting board. Once it has cooled, use your hands to break the fish into chunks.

In a serving bowl, combine the bacalao and onion. Pour in the olive oil and squeeze lemon juice over. Stir to combine well, taste for salt, and season with salt, if needed, and pepper.

Serve the ensalada immediately.

Lobster Sauce with Mofongo

Makes 1 or 2 servings

Mofongo has evolved from being served plain in a bowl—maybe with just chicken broth (my favorite way to eat it)—to being covered in all kinds of insanity, from mayoketchup or garlic cream sauce to fried pork chunks, fried chicken, stewed chicken, stewed shrimp, stewed crab, and, because it's of the era, vegan meat alternatives! When I celebrated one of my birthdays inside a liquor store in East Oakland, where La Perla Puerto Rican Cuisine once resided (they've since moved into their own brick-and-mortar), they served a lobster mofongo where the mound of tender, juicy mofongo was topped with an entire lobster tail—one of the most decadent ways that I saw mofongo being served at the time. I take the lobster meat out of the shell and roughly chop it so it's fully submerged in the sauce, but if you're cooking for company, reserve the shells to top it off.

2 tablespoons olive oil

1 yellow onion, minced

2 teaspoons garlic powder

¼ cup water

¼ cup sofrito (see page 23)

1 teaspoon fish sauce (optional)

1 Thai chile, minced (optional)

1½ pounds lobster tail meat

½ lime

Kosher salt

Freshly ground black pepper

1 recipe Mofongo (page 188)

In a skillet over medium heat, warm the olive oil. Add the onion and sauté for 2 to 5 minutes, or until browned and softened. Sprinkle in the garlic powder and cook for 2 to 3 minutes, then stir in the water and sofrito and let simmer for 3 to 5 minutes more. Add the fish sauce and chile (if using) and lobster to the sauce, stir to incorporate, and cook for 4 to 7 minutes, or until the lobster is cooked through. Squeeze lime juice into the mixture and season with salt and pepper.

Pack about ½ cup mofongo into a teacup or small bowl. Invert onto a serving plate to unmold. Repeat to make the remaining servings. Pour the lobster sauce over the mofongo and serve immediately.

Ensalada de Pulpo y Camarones

Makes 12 servings

Serve this on its own or inside coconut arepas (see page 54). If you decide to serve it with the arepas, mix the arepas dough while the octopus is cooking. Many Puerto Ricans add chunky vegetables to stretch this salad. But, since that's not my preference (and most of the vegetables that they add are the same ones in the sofrito), I just use sofrito. You can use precooked octopus if you want. It's traditional to use chopped olives and vinegar instead of lemon. The addition of cucumber is so not traditional in Puerto Rico, but the lemon and the cucumber bring a real freshness that I adore, and shrimp and cucumber is a combination that I've come to love in Mexican cooking. Sometimes I'll also add lemongrass to the boiling water.

2 garlic cloves, coarsely chopped

1 small white onion, coarsely chopped

2 dried bay leaves

1 lemon, halved, plus juice of 1 lemon

2 pounds whole octopus

1 pound 16/20-count shrimp, peeled and deveined

1 shallot, finely sliced

1 tablespoon sofrito (see page 23)

1 teaspoon olive brine

2 Persian cucumbers, coarsely chopped (optional)

Juice of 1 lime

¼ cup olive oil

Kosher salt

Fill a stockpot with water. Add the garlic, onion, bay leaves, and lemon halves and place over high heat. Bring to a rolling boil, then add the octopus, turn the heat to low, and bring to a low simmer. Cook the octopus for 45 minutes to 1 hour, or until tender when you insert a knife into the thick part of the tentacles and feel a little resistance. Add the shrimp to the pot and cook for 2 to 5 minutes, or until pink and curled.

Using tongs, remove the octopus and shrimp from the water and set aside on a cutting board until cool enough to handle. With a paring knife or kitchen scissors, remove the tentacles from the body. Alternatively, if you're more adventurous, remove and discard the head from the body, leaving the tentacles connected at the top. In the center of the tentacle bunch, there's a little circle indentation. This is the beak. Using the knife or scissors, make four slits around the indentation and pull out and discard the beak with a fork or tongs. Separate the tentacles until you have eight individual legs and roughly chop. Then chop the shrimp into pieces. Uniformity isn't incredibly important because the octopus and shrimp are already cooked.

In a serving bowl, combine the octopus and shrimp. Add the shallot, sofrito, olive brine, and cucumbers (if using). Toss to combine, then add the lemon juice, lime juice, and olive oil. Season with salt and toss again, ensuring that the dressing coats everything, then taste, adding more salt as needed.

Serve the ensalada immediately, or let chill in the fridge for up to 1 hour.

Chillo Frito

Makes 2 servings

Chillo (red snapper, sometimes written as *chio*) in Puerto Rico is one of the more common fishes that you'll see on menus. And one of the more common preparations used is . . . deep-fried. I'm not sure who decided that chillo should come only in fried mode, but I'm assuming that they thought, much like my grandmother, when in doubt . . . fry it. Puerto Ricans have mastered frying. The fish will sometimes come to your table entirely intact, its deep-fried exposed teeth and eyeballs taunting the squeamish. What the frying does is protect the fish's delicate interior texture, keeping it moist and supple and giving you the contrasting crunchy texture most humans seem to crave.

2 whole bone-in red snapper

Kosher salt

Freshly ground black pepper

6 tablespoons All-Purpose Adobo (page 20)

1 cup all-purpose flour

2 tablespoons sazón (see page 19)

Canola oil for frying

Make two to four deep vertical slits on each side of the fish; this will ensure that the flesh receives some of the seasoning and that the flesh cooks evenly and quickly. Season the fish with salt, pepper, and 3 tablespoons of the adobo, rubbing the seasoning all over, including in the slits.

On a rimmed plate, combine the flour, sazón, and remaining 3 tablespoons adobo and stir to mix. Place the seasoned fish in the flour mixture and dredge on both sides to give it a light coating of flour.

Place a wire cooling rack in a baking sheet and set near the stove. Fill a 2-quart pot or wok with 4 inches of canola oil and place over medium-high heat. You want enough oil to partially submerge the fish. Heat the oil until it registers 350°F on an instant-read thermometer. (Sprinkle in a little flour; if the oil sizzles, it's ready for frying.)

Add the fish to the oil and fry for 7 to 10 minutes on each side, or until the skin is crispy and the fish is flaking near the slits. Using tongs or a spatula, transfer the fish to the prepared rack and let cool slightly.

Serve the frito warm.

Halibut with Mojo Isleño

Makes 2 servings

Mahi-mahi, also known as *dorado* and *dolphinfish* in Puerto Rico, is the traditional fish for this recipe. But halibut and king salmon reign supreme in Northern California. Halibut and mahi-mahi have similar textures and flavors. Their fillets are thick and their taste is mild. Mahi-mahi is great when it's grilled—it collects all that char. Or you can cook it in a parchment or foil pouch with butter and lemon. Hailing from Salinas, Puerto Rico, where the sauce in this recipe was allegedly created, mojo isleño is usually served with fried fish. A similar sauce accompanies bacalao a la vizcaina, a salted cod stew with Spanish roots. But mahi-mahi is a sturdy specimen that can withstand the sometimes-cumbersome tomato sauce of mojo isleño.

Restaurant owner Eladia "Ladi" Correa of Ladi's Place claims to be the creator of this historical sauce in the late 1930s or '40s, when she modified a recipe from the Canary Islands, using local-to-her ingredients.

Salinas now has a Ruta Gastronómica del Mojo Isleño, a section of the coast dedicated to restaurants specializing in this sauce and fresh seafood, plus an international mojo isleño festival, with frenemy competitions between neighbors and barrios. The festival closes out with participants creating a massive batch of mojo isleño with a couple of cooks keeping the mixture moving, using metal oars.

¼ cup olive oil

2 (8-ounce) halibut fillets

Kosher salt

Freshly ground black pepper

4 garlic cloves, finely minced

1 medium yellow onion, sliced into thick rings

1 (8-ounce) can tomato sauce

½ cup sofrito (see page 23)

¼ cup alcaparrado

2 tablespoons sazón (see page 19)

2 cups water, or as needed

¼ cup white vinegar

Add 2 tablespoons of the olive oil to a large sauté pan and place over high heat. Add the halibut fillets and season with salt and pepper. Turn the heat to medium-high and sauté for 3 to 5 minutes on one side, then flip with a spatula, and cook the second side for 3 to 5 minutes more. Transfer the fish to a plate and set aside.

In the same sauté pan, without wiping it out, over medium-high heat, warm the remaining 2 tablespoons olive oil. Add the garlic and onion and sauté for 1 to 2 minutes. Stir in the tomato sauce, sofrito, alcaparrado, sazón, and water; turn the heat to low; and let simmer, uncovered, for 20 to 30 minutes. This transforms the tomato sauce from super-acidic to slightly sweet. Stir in the vinegar and cook for 5 to 10 minutes more. The sauce should be loose, so add more water if needed. Season with salt and pepper. Return the fish to the pan and spoon the sauce over and around, making sure it is well coated.

Serve the halibut from the pan.

Poultry

n January 2018, Puerto Ricans lost a culinary heavyweight with the passing of Adela Fargas of Casa Adela on New York's Lower East Side. Adela was born in Carolina, Puerto Rico, around 1936. Her mother worked in a bra factory in Canales, Puerto Rico, where Adela would later work part-time as a seamstress. When the factory laid them off, she began working alongside her mother by catering and selling premade lunches to factory workers. Adela moved to the United States in 1975, which would have been when she was about thirty-nine. She found herself working as a cook on the Lower East Side when the neighborhood was predominantly Puerto Rican. When her employer shut its doors, Adela hustled in la calle, selling Puerto Rican street snacks to the community. Soon after, she opened her own restaurant, where she cooked to order in a cuchifrito-land of heat-lamp and steam table–speed service.

Her restaurant started as a humble hole-in-the-wall, but over time, the original building that housed it was condemned and gutted due to substandard conditions. Fortunately, the New York City Department of Housing Preservation and Development and the Urban Homestead Program gave tenants the option of returning with the assistance of the Housing Development Fund Corporation co-op to build out their own units. So that's what Adela did. Much like the coffee shops of North Beach in San Francisco that served as havens for the beatniks once upon a time, Casa Adela served as a muse, community meeting center, and low-cost meal provider for Nuyorican poets, including Tato Laviera. Laviera even immortalized Adela's mondongo—a tripe soup—in one of his poems, "Criollo Story." In the poem, he describes the smells, tastes, and ingredients of Adela's mondongo as the cure-all to his cruda, a hangover.

In the almost folkloric work ethic of our Puerto Rican abuelas from Adela's generation, it was nothing for her to awaken at the crack of dawn to head to the restaurant. She'd start the day by cooking her pernil, a large pork shoulder that was slow-roasted until the skin became thin and crispy and refracted light like untempered glass. The meat was spoon-tender. But it was her roasted chicken for which she became famous. Patrons would drop in after work to purchase her chicken, just like countless office workers now buy a supermarket rotisserie chicken on their way home. And so, Adela would spend the day cooking with a restless affection for her craft and her gente, keeping a watchful eye on the community until she called it a night at around eleven o'clock. Many said this is how she spent her life right up until her passing.

Adela's death was a loss that came on the heels of another fallen titan a few years earlier. In 2016, Alfredo Ayala—the godfather of Puerto Rican cuisine—also died without much fanfare. Considering Alfredo was said to have taught Eric Ripert a thing or two, you'd think stateside food periodicals would have dedicated at least a paragraph to his passing. What Adela represented to the Nuyorican community, the diaspora, and Puerto Ricans is disappearing—not just in the United States but on the island as well. These days, you'd be hard-pressed to track down mondongo at many of the restaurants in Puerto Rico. At Casa Adela, Adela's daughter-in-law can now be seen working the line as head cook most nights. Whenever I'm in town, I'll stop by and just watch her through the window. A mountain of pressure must be on those shoulders, but you couldn't tell by her stoicism.

Adela was buried in her hometown of Carolina. And, so, another Puerto Rican culinary legend has left a hole in the bicultural diaspora's paradoxical need to feel connected in our world of ni de aquí, ni de allá. I hope the stories of Adela and Alfredo and their recipes help the diaspora preserve the culture for future generations.

An excerpt from "Criollo Story"

. . . i was so drunk i could not even laugh
and then salvation time
"for you, mira, mondongo"
i thought tyrone was goofing on me
"you look like a mondongo yourself"
"no, no, not you, mira, i mean, HUMERA
for HUMERA, mondongo, bro, adela,
she opens at five o'clock, let's
eat some of that tripe"
we walked into adela's five-
thirty morning mountain smell
of madrugada simmering concrete
puerto rican new york radio JIT
cuatro-music, recordado a borinquen
songs made famous by don santiago
grevi, and the crushed plantains
bollitos rounded boricua matzo all
around cleaned vinaigrette tripe
and patitas de cerdo pig feet,
softened to a melted overblown
delicacy, brother, and i tell you that
down went the russian vodka
the alcohol disappear with
bites of calabaza-pumpkin pieces
and the one hundred proof bacardi
was choked by un canto de yautia
tubers that were rooting the european
dry red wine into total decolonization
and the broth, brother, EL CALDO
condimented garlic onions
peppered with whole tomatoes
that were melted by the low

heat, ese caldo was woefully
seducing the jamaican liquors
into compatibility, and down
went the BORRACHERA, bro, and
without talking, i looked
across to tyrone's second
plate, i thanked my brother
with a smile, as we kissed
adela, and what the hell
we took the number six into
orchard beach, on section
three, and we blew the sun
as we serenaded the moon.

—Tato Laviera

Casa Adela–Inspired Roasted Chicken

Serves 4 to 6

I'd like to think that roast chicken is on most people's weekly menus either as a lazy midweek recipe or a dedicated Sunday meal. But recipes are always just suggestions, and roasted chicken recipes especially so. They leave so much room for interpretation—with citrus, herbs, and aromatics—so when someone is known for their roasted chicken, you know their recipe must be something magical.

Adela's beloved whole roasted chicken recipe wasn't traditional to Puerto Rico. There's a rumor that the rub came from a Peruano employee, but most of the seasonings are commonly found in traditional Puerto Rican recipes: vinegar, garlic, oregano, achiote, cumin. Her chicken would spend the day on a vintage rotisserie that auto-turned the bird until it was plump, juicy, and glowing.

5 garlic cloves, finely chopped

Kosher salt

1 tablespoon ground achiote

1 tablespoon paprika

2 teaspoons ground cumin

1 teaspoon dried oregano

1 tablespoon olive oil, or as needed

Freshly ground black pepper

1 tablespoon white vinegar

Juice of 1 large lemon

1 whole chicken

1 medium yellow onion, halved

Basic White Rice (page 164) for serving

Tres Hermanas Sauté (page 180) for serving

In a mortar, mash the garlic with a few pinches of salt until a paste forms. Add the achiote, paprika, cumin, oregano, and olive oil; season with pepper; and mash and mix together. Add the vinegar and half the lemon juice and mix again. Rub the mixture on the chicken, including under the skin, then pour the remaining lemon juice into the bird's cavity and insert the onion halves. Tuck the wings underneath the bird and let the chicken sit at cool room temperature for at least 1 hour or in the fridge overnight. (If the chicken is chilled, let it come to room temperature for about 30 minutes before roasting.)

Preheat the oven to 400°F.

Roast the chicken breast-side up for 30 minutes, then baste with the pan juices. If no pan juices have accumulated at this point, brush the skin with olive oil. Continue roasting the chicken, basting or brushing every 30 minutes, until its juices run clear and a thermometer inserted into the thigh registers 160°F. Depending on the size of the chicken, this will take 60 to 90 minutes. Let it rest for at least 10 minutes or until room temperature.

Carve the chicken and serve with rice and beans.

Mojo Braised Chicken

Makes 3 to 6 servings

This is one of those recipes to make when the days are too warm to turn on the oven but cool enough that you want to cozy up to a bowl of braised *something* over rice. Maybe that's just me. This recipe was developed on that type of day, toward the beginning of spring, when there were still fresh oranges on my backyard trees. Mojo is a blend of citrus and herbs that's used to marinate proteins, but it works just as well as a vehicle for braising liquid. It's not fair how little work you have to do to create a mojo compared to how much flavor mojo lends to your dishes.

1 teaspoon ground achiote

1 teaspoon ground cumin

2 teaspoons dried oregano

6 bone-in, skin-on chicken thighs

3 tablespoons olive oil

6 garlic cloves, coarsely minced

1 yellow onion, minced

Juice of 2 oranges

Juice of 1 lime

Juice of 1 lemon

Kosher salt

Freshly ground black pepper

1 bunch cilantro, coarsely chopped (optional)

In a small bowl, combine the achiote, cumin, and oregano and stir to mix. Rub the mixture over the chicken and let it marinate at cool room temperature for at least 1 hour or in the fridge overnight. (If the chicken is chilled, let it come to room temperature for about 30 minutes before roasting.)

Add 1 tablespoon of the olive oil to a skillet and place over medium-low heat. Add the garlic and onion and let them sweat for 30 seconds to 1 minute, or until translucent. Transfer the garlic-onion mixture to a small bowl and set aside.

Without wiping out the skillet, add the remaining 2 tablespoons olive oil and turn the heat to high. When the oil is hot, add the chicken skin-side down and sear for 4 to 5 minutes, or until brown. Add the garlic-onion mixture, orange juice, lime juice, and lemon juice to the pan and turn the heat to low. Bring to a simmer and braise, uncovered, for 20 to 30 minutes, or until the chicken is cooked all the way through. Season with salt and pepper.

Garnish the chicken with the cilantro, if desired, and serve immediately.

Chicharron de Pollo

Makes 4 servings

You're confused, I know. By now you've been eating chicharrones for years, always in the form of soft, airy pork rinds from the corner store or the hard, crunchy variety with some fat attached that you bought at the Mexican market. Am I right? Puerto Ricans call their fried chicken *chicharron* because it's fried "hard," until the exterior is as crispy as a chicharron. But that applies only to chicken. If you take pork chunks and fry them hard, those are called *carne frita*. For years, my grandma would make large holiday meals for the family—big pots of rice, fried fritters, and lots of pork at the center of it all. My uncle Darrell didn't eat swine, so my grandma always made him his own special fried chicken. And no one else touched it until Uncle Darrell left the townhouse and we knew for sure he'd had his fill. The chicken was always in whole pieces (it's usually cut up into small chunks), sunburnt brown on the outside, crunchy as can be, a little blackened from cooking too hot on the bottom of the cast-iron skillet, and almost always still pink in the center. My grandma was a good cook, but fried chicken was her nemesis. However, you'd never know. Uncle Darrell never once complained. He happily ate the fried chicken until he reached the inedible raw part and then he moved on to another piece. There's only one other place that I've ever been served chicharron de pollo in whole pieces and that's at El Coqui Puerto Rican Cuisine in Santa Rosa, California.

4 large boneless, skin-on chicken thighs

Kosher salt

Freshly ground black pepper

2 tablespoons garlic powder

2 tablespoons onion powder

1 tablespoon sazón (see page 19)

1 teaspoon ground cumin

2 cups all-purpose flour

1 tablespoon paprika

Canola oil for frying

Sauce of your choosing, such as mayoketchup (see page 20), for serving

Cut the chicken into 2-inch pieces, leaving the skin on. Season the chicken with salt, pepper, 1 tablespoon of the garlic powder, 1 tablespoon of the onion powder, sazón, and cumin. Set aside.

In a shallow bowl, combine the remaining 1 tablespoon garlic powder, remaining 1 tablespoon onion powder, flour, and paprika. Season with salt and pepper and mix well. Add the seasoned chicken and toss gently to coat.

Place a wire cooling rack in a baking sheet and set near the stove. Fill a 12-inch cast-iron skillet with 3 inches of canola oil and place over medium-high heat. You want enough oil to cover the chicken halfway. Heat the oil until it registers 350°F on an instant-read thermometer. (Sprinkle in a little flour; if the oil sizzles, it's ready for frying.)

Remove chicken pieces from the seasoned flour, shaking off excess flour. Add half the chicken to the oil and fry for 5 to 7 minutes, or until golden brown. Using tongs, flip the pieces and fry for 5 to 7 minutes more. Transfer the chicken to the prepared rack. Repeat with the remaining chicken pieces.

Serve the chicken immediately with sauce on the side.

Mami's Mushroom Chicken

Makes 4 servings

Mushroom chicken is my favorite childhood dish and Mom's specialty. It's one that's umami-heavy: meaty, earthy, dark. My mom doesn't cook much these days, opting to use our joint third-party delivery app to have Chinese food delivered to her wrought-iron fence. But if I give her puppy eyes and ask her to make this for me, she'll send me to the store to gather the ingredients. It's one of the simplest things to assemble, and even though I have watched her make it, I can never get mine to taste the same as hers. My mother is calm, patient, and approachable. I am skittish and make babies cry. Maybe it's these differences that are the reason I cannot duplicate this damn dish! I asked my mom to cook mushroom chicken so I could chronicle the recipe for the book. We sat down to eat afterward, and when I took my first bite, the crust of the chicken was so crispy it shattered. My mom looked up at me and said, "Hear it?"

3 tablespoons salted butter

8 ounces cremini mushrooms, sliced

8 chicken wings

Kosher salt

Freshly ground black pepper

1 cup all-purpose flour, plus 1 tablespoon

Canola oil for frying

1 (10½-ounce) can cream of mushroom soup

1⅓ cups milk

Soy sauce (preferably Kikkoman) for seasoning

Basic White Rice (page 164) for serving

Add 2 tablespoons of the butter to a large skillet and place over medium-high heat. Add the mushrooms and sauté for 8 to 10 minutes, or until they've released and reabsorbed their moisture. Set aside.

Season the chicken wings with salt and pepper. Place the 1 cup flour in a shallow bowl and dredge the chicken in the flour.

Line a plate with paper towels and set near the stove. Fill a 12-inch cast-iron skillet a little less than halfway with canola oil and place over medium-high heat. You want enough oil to cover the chicken. Heat the oil until it registers 350°F on an instant-read thermometer. (Sprinkle in a little flour; if the oil sizzles, it's ready for frying.)

Add the chicken to the oil in two batches and fry for 10 to 12 minutes, or until it is like fried chicken. (It doesn't matter if it's cooked all the way through, it'll finish cooking in the mushroom sauce.) Using tongs, transfer the chicken to the prepared plate. Pour out most of the oil in the pan, leaving a tablespoon or so.

Turn the heat to low and add the 1 tablespoon flour, remaining 1 tablespoon butter, and mushroom soup to the pan. Whisk vigorously for 1 minute, then whisk in the milk. If the mixture's too thick (it starts to stick to the bottom of the pan), add a bit of water. If it's too loose (not clinging to the spoon), turn the heat to medium and simmer until slightly thickened. It should look like an old-fashioned country gravy. Add a few shakes of soy sauce, then while the mixture is simmering and when you see little bubbles, add the mushrooms and chicken, submerging as much of them as you can. Turn the heat to low and let simmer, stirring occasionally and making sure the gravy doesn't stick to the bottom of the pan, for 15 minutes.

Serve the mushroom chicken over rice.

Pinchos with Guava BBQ Sauce

Makes 6 servings

Mami and I knew we were officially lost as we drove down the Carretera 2, cutting through Manatí, when we saw the Walmart. We turned off the main highway. And turned. And turned. Finally, my mom spotted a trailer on the side of the road. It was hoisted on cinder blocks with a sign out front: PINCHOS DE POLLO 3x5$. Before I knew it, my mom had power-walked toward the trailer. When the vendor saw us, he pulled a couple of marinated chicken skewers out of his Cambro food carrier and set them over the charcoal grill. The chicken danced and sizzled as it turned Hawaiian Tropic gold. He then slathered the skewers in quintessential Puerto Rican guava BBQ sauce, and the sugars immediately started to caramelize and pop, lacquering the chicken. He placed a slice of French bread on top of each skewer and handed them to us. The chicken was thick and luscious, sweet, tangy, and sharp, the guava sauce a perfect counter to the rich dark meat. This is my genuflection to that vendor; my recipe is bright with fresh citrus, spicy with sriracha, and complex with fish sauce.

Juice of 1 lime

½ cup orange juice

2 tablespoons sazón (see page 19)

2 tablespoons mixed herb blend (such as Mrs. Dash Table Blend or Trader Joe's 21 Seasoning Salute)

Kosher salt

6 boneless, skinless chicken thighs

Guava BBQ Sauce

2 cups ketchup

¼ cup water

¼ cup packed light brown sugar

2 tablespoons apple cider vinegar

2 tablespoons lemon juice

1 tablespoon soy sauce

1 tablespoon fish sauce

1 tablespoon chili-garlic sauce

1 tablespoon sriracha

1 tablespoon onion powder

5 garlic cloves, finely minced

1 cup guava paste (from a concentrated block), cut into small pieces

6 slices French bread

In a large bowl, combine the lime juice, orange juice, sazón, and herb blend; season with salt; and stir to mix into a marinade.

Cut each chicken thigh into eight cubes, adding to the bowl of marinade as you go. When all the chicken has been cut, massage the marinade into the chicken. Let marinate at cool room temperature for 1 hour or in the fridge for up to overnight.

Preheat a grill to medium-hot. Soak six wooden skewers in water for 30 minutes.

To make the sauce: In a medium saucepan over low heat, combine the ketchup, water, brown sugar, vinegar, lemon juice, soy sauce, fish sauce, chili-garlic sauce, sriracha, onion powder, garlic, and guava paste and bring to a simmer. Let simmer for 3 to 5 minutes.

Thread eight chicken cubes onto each skewer. Grill the chicken for 15 minutes, then lightly bathe the skewers in BBQ sauce and cook for 5 minutes more. Slather with another coat of sauce and cook for an additional 5 minutes. The sauce should be slightly charred.

Cap each skewer with a slice of French bread and serve immediately.

Pavochon

Makes 8 to 12 servings

Pavochon, both the word and the dish, is one of Puerto Rico's many Spanglish creations. A mash-up of *pavo* for "turkey" and *chon* for "lechón," it has become the centerpiece of Puerto Rican Thanksgiving. Come November, supermarket shelves across Puerto Rico hold all the classic components: cranberry sauce, stuffing, dinner rolls. The diaspora became accustomed to these items Stateside and brought them back to the island—which could be how pavochon was born.

1 (12- to 14-pound) whole turkey, neck and giblets removed and reserved, and the bird patted dry

1 lemon, halved

Kosher salt

Freshly ground black pepper

3 tablespoons unsalted butter, at room temperature

¼ cup extra-virgin olive oil

3 tablespoons achiote paste

2 tablespoons dried oregano

2 tablespoons granulated garlic

2 teaspoons ground cumin

1 large yellow onion, halved

5 garlic cloves

2 celery stalks

1½ cups water, or as needed

2 cups chicken stock

Using your fingers, and starting at the neck, gently separate the turkey skin from the breast meat. Rub the outside of the turkey all over with the lemon; set the lemon aside. Season the bird inside and out with salt (be generous) and pepper. Rub the butter over the breast meat and underneath the skin.

In a small bowl, combine the olive oil, achiote paste, oregano, granulated garlic, and cumin and mash to form a smooth paste. Rub the paste all over the outside of the turkey in an even layer. Tie the legs together with kitchen twine and let sit at room temperature for 2 hours, or place on a wire cooking rack set inside a rimmed baking sheet and chill, uncovered, in the fridge for up to 2 days. (If the turkey is chilled, let it sit at room temperature for 1 hour before roasting.)

Position a rack in the bottom third of the oven and preheat to 450°F. Set a clean wire cooling rack or V-shaped roasting rack in a large roasting pan.

Place the onion, garlic cloves, celery, and reserved lemon inside the turkey cavity (or tuck some alongside the turkey). Place the turkey on the prepared rack and pour the water into the pan. Roast the turkey for 25 to 30 minutes, rotating once if it is browning unevenly, until the skin is browned all over and beginning to crisp. Turn the oven temperature to 350°F and continue to roast (and rotate the pan) about 1½ hours more, basting the turkey with the pan juices every 30 minutes and adding more water, ½ cup at a time, if it completely evaporates, until an instant-read thermometer inserted into the thickest part of the breast registers 150° to 155°F, and the thickest part of a thigh registers 165° to 170°F. Transfer the turkey to a carving board and let rest for 30 to 60 minutes.

Remove the rack and place the roasting pan over medium heat. Add the chicken stock and deglaze, using a wooden spoon to scrape the bottom of the pan to loosen any browned bits. Cook for 1 to 2 minutes and then transfer to a small pitcher or bowl.

Carve the turkey and serve with the pan sauce to spoon over.

Calle del Cristo Street Marker,
Old San Juan, Puerto Rico.

Capilla del Cristo,
Old San Juan, Puerto Rico.

Catedral de San Juan Bautista,
Old San Juan, Puerto Rico.

Thanksgiving Leftovers Pavochon Pasta Bake

Makes 4 servings

Thanksgiving doesn't look the way it did when I was a kid in a tiny townhouse crammed with people who both loved and hated each other. These days, Thanksgiving is usually just Mami and me. The COVID pandemic prevented a lot of folks from seeing their loved ones and celebrating Thanksgiving in their traditional way, and that made me realize that not everyone is used to a Thanksgiving that consists of two people. But that didn't stop many of us from making a big ol' bird. This recipe is actually something that I just came up with and I make for myself every post-Thanksgiving. It wasn't ever a *real* recipe, but I made it one just for you.

8 ounces dried rigatoni

2 tablespoons salted butter

2 tablespoons all-purpose flour

4 cups milk

2 tablespoons Illyanna's Adobo (page 20)

1 cup Mexican-style shredded cheese blend

½ cup grated Parmesan cheese

Kosher salt

Freshly ground black pepper

3 cups coarsely chopped light- and dark-meat turkey

Maisonet's Cornbread and Salami Dressing (page 190) for serving

Olive oil for drizzling

Preheat the oven to 400°F.

Bring a large pot of salted water to a boil. Add the rigatoni and boil until al dente. Using a glass measuring cup, scoop out 2½ cups of the pasta water, then drain the rigatoni and set aside.

In the same pot over medium heat, melt the butter. Stir in the flour and cook for about 1 minute, until it has turned golden brown. Slowly whisk in 2 cups of the reserved pasta water, ensuring that the mixture is thickened before you continue. If it looks thin, let it simmer until thickened, about 2 minutes. If it's too thick, stir in enough of the remaining ½ cup pasta water to thin. Whisk in the milk and let simmer to thicken. Stir in the adobo, then add both cheeses and mix well. Season with salt and pepper.

Add the turkey and rigatoni to the pot and stir to combine well, ensuring everything is covered in the sauce. Transfer the mixture to a 9 by 13-inch baking pan with high sides. Spoon the dressing over the top and drizzle a little olive oil over the dressing. Bake the casserole for 20 to 40 minutes, until you smell it.

Spoon the pasta bake onto plates and serve hot.

Note: If the consistency of your sauce isn't thick, you can add a cornstarch slurry by dissolving 1 teaspoon cornstarch in 1 tablespoon room-temperature water and adding it after you add the milk. I always have to do this because I don't have the patience to wait for the sauce to thicken on its own.

Pork

h, pork. Monarch of colonial proteins. Seen in many of our celebratory foods, pork is king in Puerto Rico. But not because it was native to the culture, as documented in Columbus's journal: "Beasts, we saw none, nor any creatures on land save parrots and lizards, but a boy told me he saw a large snake. No sheep nor goats were seen, and although our stay here has been short, it being now noon, yet were there any, I could hardly have failed of seeing them." As far as Columbus was concerned, this land required everything—everything that the colonists were going to need to supply their long-term stay.

One of those resources was livestock, including pigs. Hogs first came ashore with Columbus. The documentation shows that a total of 118 pigs were brought to San Juan in 1512; in 1513, another 273 pigs arrived. They quickly adapted to the environment, became a source of food for the enslaved Tainos, and throughout history have been readily available through economic and demographic changes. And, possibly, they were also in demand after people developed a taste for their rich meat.

Burnt sienna–hued suckling pigs can be seen on their spits all along the Ruta de Lechón in the Guavate barrio of Cayey—an entire area where lechoneros/as specialize and compete in roasting hogs to perfection. Visitors coming to the island might return home and tell their friends and family that Puerto Ricans love pork. Do we? Or is it simply one of the few proteins that we are allowed under the strict government rules and guidelines?

Jamonilla Guisada

Makes 4 servings

This is a post–World War II creation, consisting of tomato sauce, sofrito, canned vegetables, and Spam. Like a number of Puerto Rican recipes, it was born from the island's historical collision between government-imposed food sanctions and the imperative to make something out of nothing, and it has since become a mainstay in many kitchens through a combination of nostalgia and genuine fondness. And if Puerto Rican food should have long ago been included in the United States' repertoire—after all, Puerto Rico *is* part of the United States—then Spam guisada is a dish whose simplicity and reliance on pantry staples illustrate why now is a good time to start appreciating the island's recipes.

¼ cup canola oil

1 small yellow onion, julienned

Kosher salt

5 garlic cloves, coarsely chopped

2 cups water

¼ cup tomato sauce

2 tablespoons sofrito (see page 23)

2 tablespoons sazón (see page 19)

1 medium russet potato, cut into medium dice

Freshly ground black pepper

1 tablespoon mixed herb blend (such as Mrs. Dash Table Blend or Trader Joe's 21 Seasoning Salute)

1 (12-ounce) can Spam Classic, cut into medium dice

1 (15-ounce) can corn kernels, drained

1 (15-ounce) can green beans, drained

Basic White Rice (page 164) for serving

Add 2 tablespoons of the canola oil to a 10-inch skillet and place over medium heat. When the oil is shimmering, add the onion, season with salt, and sauté for 1 to 2 minutes. Add the garlic and sauté for 1 to 2 minutes more, or until translucent. Stir in the water, tomato sauce, sofrito, and sazón. Transfer the tomato mixture to a bowl and set aside.

In the same pan, without wiping it out, over medium heat, warm the remaining 2 tablespoons canola oil. Add the potato and season with salt, pepper, and the herb blend. Sauté the potato 2 to 3 minutes, or until browned. Add the Spam and sauté for 2 to 3 minutes more, or until browned, then add the tomato mixture. Turn the heat to low and let simmer for 10 to 15 minutes, or until the potato is soft and fork-tender.

Spoon a few of the potato pieces into a bowl, mash, and add back to the pot to ensure that the mixture thickens. Stir in the corn and green beans and let simmer for 5 minutes, or until the vegetables are warmed through.

Serve the guisada with scoops of rice.

Nana's Oven-Barbecued Ribs

Makes 4 to 6 servings

I don't remember if Nana had a grill or not. But I definitely remember these ribs. The image of Nana opening the oven door and pulling out a large and blackened roasting pan, the ribs floating in an insane amount of oil, is both horrifying and comforting. I never knew how Nana could coax oil out of a rock. And, somehow, she did. The loose sauce makes the eating experience much better, if messier, and these ribs are perfect for serving over rice.

1 tablespoon All-Purpose Adobo (page 20)

2 pounds pork spareribs

Kosher salt

Freshly ground black pepper

½ cup water, or as needed

Barbecue Sauce

1 cup ketchup

2 tablespoons water

2 tablespoons light brown sugar

1 tablespoon white vinegar

½ tablespoon soy sauce

½ tablespoon fish sauce

½ tablespoon sriracha

2 thin slices lemon

Basic White Rice (page 164) for serving

Preheat the oven to 350°F. Line a roasting pan with aluminum foil.

Rub the adobo all over the spareribs and season generously with salt and pepper. Place the ribs in the prepared roasting pan, then pour in the water and cover tightly with foil. Roast for 1½ hours, or until the meat is tender.

To make the barbecue sauce: In a small pot over medium high heat, combine the ketchup, water, brown sugar, vinegar, soy sauce, fish sauce, and sriracha. Let simmer until the sauce is thick and bubbling. Add the lemon slices and stir.

Uncover the ribs and pour the barbecue sauce into the pan, ensuring that all the ribs are coated in sauce. Re-cover with the foil and roast for 1 to 2 hours more, or until the sauce has started to thicken and latch on to the ribs. If the sauce starts to thicken too much, add some water to the pan to loosen up. You want these to be on the saucy side.

Cut the ribs into pieces and serve over rice.

Puerto Rican Laab

Makes 2 or 3 servings

For as much as I have yelled at people on social media about not using the terms *homage* or *inspired by*, you'd think that I would have never committed this crime. And yet, here we are. It's a long story, but you already know it if you've been following my journey; I lived with a Laotian family in my teens. I don't want to get into details because they're essentially meaningless regarding this bastardization of laap. This recipe is from my memory of how my Lao family made the dish and the flavors that satisfy my own cravings. I use padaek (a much thicker, more seasoned, and pungent sibling of fish sauce) because it's a Laotian ingredient and the Saigon (also known as Super) brand because they're what I saw being used when laab was made at home. I don't know enough about Laotian food to have other preferences when it comes to ingredients. I just stick to what I saw when I lived with my Lao family, the Khamsalys.

2 tablespoons canola oil

1 pound ground pork

1 large shallot, coarsely sliced

5 garlic cloves, coarsely chopped

2 Thai chiles, coarsely chopped

1 cup fresh green beans

2 tablespoons toasted rice powder

¼ cup sofrito (see page 23)

⅓ cup fish sauce (preferably Squid brand)

2 tablespoons granulated sugar

3 tablespoons padaek (preferably Saigon/Super brand)

2 limes; 1 halved, 1 cut into wedges

1 bunch cilantro, coarsely chopped

1 bunch mint, coarsely chopped

1 bunch basil, coarsely chopped

1 head iceberg, bibb, or romaine lettuce, leaves separated

1 bunch radishes, thinly sliced

1 cucumber, thinly sliced

Add the canola oil to a large skillet and place over medium heat. When the oil is hot, add the pork and sauté for 2 to 3 minutes, add the shallot and sauté for 1 minute, then add the garlic and chiles and sauté for 2 minutes more. Stir in the green beans and sauté for 1 minute, then stir in the toasted rice powder and sofrito and cook for 1 minute. Stir in the fish sauce and cook for 1 minute, then stir in the sugar and cook for 1 minute more. Add the padaek, stir to incorporate, and cook for 1 minute.

Squeeze the juice of the lime halves over the mixture. Stir in half of the cilantro, mint, and basil, reserving the remainder of each for serving. Transfer the pork mixture into a serving bowl.

Place the lettuce leaves, remaining herbs, lime wedges, radishes, and cucumber on a serving plate. Spoon the pork mixture into a lettuce leaf and top with some herbs, cucumber, radishes, and a squeeze of lime. Fold closed and eat.

Pernil

Makes 8 to 10 servings

Every December 24, our phone would ring at the ass-crack of dawn—and we always knew who it was. It was Nana, threatening to never cook Christmas dinner again if we didn't come over immediately and help her remove the beast of a pork roast from the oven. And without fail, we'd show up to her townhouse in the ten minutes it took to drive the one mile from our house, and there'd be ten other people standing in the kitchen to help her take the roast out of the oven. One, she called everyone so *someone* would show up. Two, it was a tool of manipulation to ensure that everyone (even those who were currently beefing with each other) would be under one roof for the holidays. Pretty sneaky, Sis. But there was nothing like that smell of garlic and oregano bitch-slapping you in the face as soon as you walked through the door. And there was nothing like seeing that glorious roast beast ascending from the oven. The skin glistened and was shatteringly crispy: you could hear it crackling from having all its fat rendered.

This two-day method is one of my nana's recipes that I don't stray from. I puncture the pork shoulder all over and insert a gargantuan number of whole garlic cloves into each slit. I rub the pork with a mixture of olive oil, sazón, and heaps of oregano. I purchase my pork shoulder only at the same neighborhood market where my grandma purchased hers. And I make pernil only for Christmas. Nothing reminds me of my grandma more—and nothing brings me to tears quicker—than the smell of rendered pork fat, oregano, and garlic as it fills up the house. It takes 6 to 7 hours to cook pernil, largely unattended, plus the time to marinate overnight. You can cover and store leftovers in the fridge for up to 5 days, and use it to make sandwiches (see page 120).

1 (7- to 9-pound) bone-in pork shoulder or butt

10 to 15 garlic cloves

1 tablespoon olive oil

2 tablespoons dried oregano

2 tablespoons sazón (see page 19)

Kosher salt

Freshly ground black pepper

The night before cooking, using a small paring knife, poke ten to fifteen holes in the pork shoulder and stuff a garlic clove into each one. Rub the olive oil all over the pork, then thoroughly massage the shoulder with the oregano and sazón. Season liberally with salt and pepper. Place the pork in a roasting pan and refrigerate, uncovered, overnight.

Preheat the oven to 300°F.

Roast the pork shoulder, basting every hour, for 5 to 6 hours, or until the meat is very tender. Then turn the oven temperature to 400°F, arrange the pork shoulder skin-side up, and roast for 1 hour more.

Let the pork rest for about 15 minutes, giving the skin a chance to crisp. Cut into large chunks, but please don't finely shred the pork.

Serve the pernil immediately.

Leftover Pernil Sandwiches

Makes 2 sandwiches

This is just another one of those non-recipe recipes that I make for myself when I have pernil left over. There's nothing special about it, and yet whenever I serve it to people, they seem to think it's amazing. Some would probably look at this recipe and say, "It's a Cubano." But I don't use pickles or Cuban bread. And I don't even know what condiments go on a Cubano. I just combine a mixture of mustard, mayo, and sour cream (a special sauce that Mami uses for her taco burger; a burger patty stuffed into a folded flour tortilla with lettuce, shredded cheese, Parmesan cheese, and the sauce). I'm not a huge fan of mayo, but it's necessary to produce a sort of richness, and the sour cream cuts that with its tanginess.

$\frac{1}{2}$ **cup yellow mustard**

$\frac{1}{2}$ **cup mayonnaise**

$\frac{1}{2}$ **cup sour cream**

Hot sauce for seasoning

2 bolillos, Vietnamese baguettes, or sub sandwich rolls (such as Francisco Sweet French Sandwich Rolls)

$\frac{1}{4}$ **cup salted butter, at room temperature**

2 tablespoons granulated garlic

2 cups coarsely chopped Pernil (page 119)

4 slices thick country ham

2 cups coarsely shredded Mexican 4-cheese-blend mix (such as Tillamook)

In a small bowl, stir together the mustard, mayonnaise, and sour cream and season with hot sauce. Set aside.

Spread one of the sandwich rolls with 2 tablespoons of the butter, sprinkle the butter with 1 tablespoon of the granulated garlic, and then toast the bread in a skillet or on a comal over medium-high heat. Repeat with the other roll. Set aside.

In a cast-iron skillet over medium-high heat, crisp up the pernil and ham, until warmed through. Stack the pernil on the ham and top with 1 cup of the cheese.

Slather the mustard mixture on both sides of the rolls. Load the pernil, ham, and another $\frac{1}{2}$ cup cheese onto each roll. Close the sandwiches and place one back in the skillet or on the comal. Take the cast-iron skillet (in which you warmed the pernil and ham) and place it on top of the sandwich, so it squishes the sandwich down. (You can also do this step in a panini press or use a foil-wrapped brick to make sure the sandwich is pressed and becomes crispy and thin.) Carefully turn the sandwich to toast the other side. Repeat to make the second sandwich.

Serve the sandwiches immediately.

Leftover Pernil Cheat Chile Verde

Makes 3 or 4 servings

Sometimes I wonder why I even have to write a recipe for these non-recipes. It's mostly so you get an idea of how I eat at home and use leftovers. But it's kind of funny because it also reminds me of the types of semi-homemade shortcuts that Mami would make when trying to work a full-time job and get dinner on the table for her cherub of a child. Sometimes, during summer months, I'll doctor up a jarred chile verde sauce by fortifying it with roasted garlic, roasted peppers, and roasted onions, giving it a more chill aspect as opposed to its own zingy flavor. Still, on the days when you're too tired but still want something comforting, the jar works just fine. Instead of spooning onto tortillas, you could also serve this over rice.

2 tablespoons canola oil

1 medium yellow onion, coarsely chopped

5 garlic cloves, coarsely minced

5 to 6 cups coarsely chopped Pernil (page 119)

1 (16-ounce) jar salsa verde

1 cup sofrito (see page 23)

Kosher salt

Freshly ground black pepper

Warm flour tortillas for serving

Add the canola oil to a cast-iron skillet and place over medium heat. Add the onion and sauté for 1 to 2 minutes. Add the garlic and sauté 1 minute more, then stir in the pernil, salsa verde, and sofrito. Season with salt and pepper, turn the heat to low, and let simmer until warmed through.

Spoon the chile verde onto tortillas and serve immediately.

Sandwiches de Mezcla

Makes 4 sandwiches

There are some Puerto Rican recipes that I'll just never come to enjoy. Like the comingling of canned cheese and mayonnaise. Why, lord, why? But those who like pimento cheese might enjoy its tropical cousin, mezcla. This seemingly innocent concoction makes appearances at any fancy Puerto Rican party or high tea—a sludgy, unnatural coral-colored schmear on the unholiest of white breads. And then people have the audacity to cut the entire thing into triangles with the crusts removed. This recipe makes about 4 cups of mezcla. Instead of mayo, I use mascarpone. Instead of Wonder Bread, I use rustic country bread for texture.

Mezcla

1 (15-ounce) can or jar of your favorite nacho cheese sauce or dip (I prefer La Preferida Zesty Nacho Cheese Sauce)

4 ounces mascarpone cheese

½ cup pimientos, stemmed and finely diced

1 (12-ounce) can Spam Classic or other canned meat, coarsely chopped

1 tablespoon granulated garlic

1 tablespoon granulated onion

Freshly ground black pepper

8 slices great-quality, crusty rustic bread

Butter for spreading, at room temperature

4 handfuls melty white cheese (optional)

To make the mezcla: In a food processor, combine the nacho cheese sauce, mascarpone, pimientos, Spam, granulated garlic, and granulated onion; season with pepper; and blitz for 3 minutes, or until creamy and smooth.

Place a cast-iron skillet over medium heat.

Spread one side of each bread slice with butter. Working with two slices at a time, schmear whatever quantity of mezcla that your heart desires onto the unbuttered side of a piece of bread, end to end. Top with a handful of melty white cheese (if using) and close with the other piece of bread, buttered-side up.

Place the sandwich in the skillet and toast for 2 to 5 minutes, or until the bread is thoroughly browned. Flip and repeat. Make sure the cheese on the inside is melted and the mezcla is hot, 2 to 5 minutes more. Transfer to a plate and repeat to make the other sandwiches.

Cut the sandwiches in half and serve immediately.

Note: If you have leftover mezcla, it's delicious as a dip for chips!

Chuletas

Makes 4 servings

I don't fry much at home. And I don't eat pork chops much, even though they're delicious. Most people don't seem to think that the breed of pig matters. Rancho Llano Seco sent me a care package at the beginning of the COVID pandemic, and it had been so long since I'd had a pork chop that I couldn't tell if I'd just forgotten how delicious they were or if the product was truly magical. Their pigs are a cross of Duroc, Yorkshire, and Landrace breeds. They're fed from grain and legumes that are grown a few miles away. They have constant access to the pastures, where they semi-roam their pocket of Butte County in Northern California. They were the most tender pork chops I'd ever had. Even after frying them "hard" (because Mami likes her meats to surpass well-done), they were still tender. I salivate just thinking about them. Rancho Llano Seco has found a faithful member of the congregation. I double up the seasonings in the recipe so you can easily keep them separate and use for both dredging and on the meat. It's not traditional to dredge the pork chops, but this is the way I like them.

8 thin-cut pork chops, bone-in or boneless

3 tablespoons ground achiote

3 tablespoons granulated garlic

3 tablespoons granulated onion

2 teaspoons ground cumin

2 teaspoons dried oregano

Kosher salt

Freshly ground black pepper

2 cups all-purpose flour

1 tablespoon paprika

Canola oil for frying

Flaky sea salt

Place the pork chops in a bowl and season with 1½ tablespoons of the achiote, 1½ tablespoons of the granulated garlic, 1½ tablespoons of the granulated onion, 1 teaspoon of the cumin, the oregano, kosher salt, and pepper. Set aside.

In a shallow bowl, combine the flour, paprika, remaining 1½ tablespoons achiote, remaining 1½ tablespoons granulated garlic, remaining 1½ tablespoons granulated onion, and remaining 1 teaspoon cumin; season with kosher salt and pepper; and stir to incorporate.

Dredge the pork chops in the flour mixture, ensuring that both sides are well coated. The coating can be as thick or thin as you want it. (Sometimes I'll add a few drops of water to the dredging mixture as I go along to create these little jaggedy crumbs that fry up nicely.)

Place a wire cooling rack in a baking sheet and set near the stove. Fill a large cast-iron skillet with ½ inch of canola oil and place over medium heat. Place the pork chops in the pan and fry for 2 to 3 minutes per side, or until they're golden brown and crispy. Using tongs or a spatula, transfer the chops to the prepared rack. Lightly season with flaky salt.

Serve the chuletas immediately.

Chuleta Kan-Kan

Makes 2 to 4 servings

This unusual cut of pork is elusive, which might have something to do with it being unequivocally Puerto Rican. There's some contention about who birthed it, but most seem to agree that this pork cudgel was brought forth by Don Juan Vera Martínez, owner of La Guardarraya, a restaurant that opened in the 1950s and sits on the border of Yauco and Guayanilla. The folklore behind the creation of the "can-can" is that it's named after the frilly, ruffled petticoats that women wore at the time, back when the petticoats were ironed with starch and made a distinct sound as the women walked. Find that hard to believe? Me too. What's not hard to believe is that this cut was specifically requested one day from a regular patron who wanted something special and different—a country-style pork chop with the skin still attached. What the world received, without knowing it, is a waxing/waning crescent of pork that includes loin, ribs, belly, and some skin. To make it, deep cuts are sliced along the rainbow of fat. Then the whole thing is deep-fried, and the cuts separate and flare as they turn a rich sienna brown and transform into chicharron.

Because the different types of muscles in this cut require different cooking times to achieve the best texture, this recipe ain't for the faint of heart. Eric Rivera, of Addo in Seattle, rubs his own special blend of sazón onto the meat before aging it for an unmentionable amount of time. He cooks it at 145°F for 45 minutes, chills it overnight, and then pan-fries it. I've seen these chops roasted and then fried, simmered and then fried, and sometimes just . . . straight-up fried. And while I tried all these methods for this book, the one that ultimately seemed to make the most sense for a home cook is the simmer-and-fry method.

Kan-Kan Marinade

2 tablespoons minced fresh garlic

1 tablespoon All-Purpose Adobo (page 20)

1 tablespoon ground achiote

1 teaspoon dried oregano

1 teaspoon ground cumin

¼ to ⅓ cup olive oil

Kosher salt

Freshly ground black pepper

2 pounds country-style pork chops

Canola oil for frying

To make the marinade: In a small bowl, combine the garlic, adobo, achiote, oregano, cumin, and enough of the olive oil to make a loose mixture. Season with salt and pepper.

Make deep slits in the entire length of the fat on the chops, then rub the meat with the marinade. Set aside at cool room temperature for at least 1 hour or in the fridge for as long as overnight.

Transfer the chops and any marinade that clings to them to a large pot and place over low heat. Add just enough water to cover the chops, bring to a simmer, and cook for 40 minutes to 1 hour, or until the meat is tender. Remove the chops from the water, pat dry, and set aside.

continued ▶

Chuleta Kan-Kan, continued

Place a wire cooling rack in a baking sheet and set near the stove. Fill a 2-quart pot with 4 to 5 inches of canola oil and place over medium-high heat. You want enough oil to deep-fry the chops. Heat the oil until it registers 350°F on an instant-read thermometer.

Place the chops in the oil and fry for 25 to 30 minutes, or until the fat has rendered and chicharroned. Using tongs, transfer the chops to the prepared rack to drain.

Serve the chuleta hot.

Pasteles

Makes 18 to 24 pasteles

Possibly pre-Columbian, this is one of Puerto Rico's oldest recipes. *Aguinaldo*, published in 1893, is a collection of poems, essays, and stories by various Puerto Rican poets and authors. It was in this book that Francisco Vassallo Forés briefly mentions an account of pasteles when he describes a festive Christmas night feast: "... pues qué? dejaremos escapar cobardemente de nuestras manos el puerquito asado de Noche Buena, el arroz con melao (arroz con dulce), LOS PASTELES DE HOJA, el queso, arroz con perico, y demás manjares, TODAVÍA EN VIGOR EN NUESTROS CAMPOS."

My family wraps their pasteles in foil. That's right. I said it. Little did I know how controversial this would be until I posted a video of Mami making them one Christmas. So many self-righteous Puerto Ricans on the internet shouted, "Those are not pasteles!" Actually, they are. Much in the same way there are pasteles de arroz de Corozal and pasteles de yuca, you should think of our family's pasteles as pasteles de California. When you think of my grandma coming to Sacramento as a seventeen-year-old mother of two in 1956, you have to wonder where the hell would she have found banana leaves in Northern California?! She met the real test of preserving her heritage by giving a shit about adapting in an effort to see the legacy of her homeland's food live on. Grandma kept calm, used what was readily available—aluminum foil—and carried on. Sometimes I think some Puerto Ricans would rather see the foods of the island disappear than adapt to geography and necessity.

Kosher salt

1 small yautía blanca (also sold as white malanga)

½ small russet potato

12 guineos, peeled (see page 12)

1 super-firm plátano, peeled (see page 12)

4 cups achiote oil (see page 19)

1 recipe Carne Guisada (page 151), braising liquid included, at room temperature

Cut eighteen to twenty-four 12-inch squares of aluminum foil. Prepare a large bowl of cold water and add a large handful of salt. Set everything aside.

Peel the skins from the yautía and potato and add the flesh to the prepared guineos and plátano. Set aside.

Place a box grater in a large bowl. Using the side with the smallest holes (the ones that protrude outward and are spiky), grate the guineos, plátano, yautía, and potato and season with salt. This is your masa.

Using a spoon, make a well in the middle of the masa. Gradually pour ½ cup of the achiote oil into the well and, using the spoon, quickly and carefully fold the oil into the masa. Add another ½ cup achiote oil and keep folding until all the oil has been absorbed and the masa has turned from Silly Putty brown to reddish orange.

continued ▶

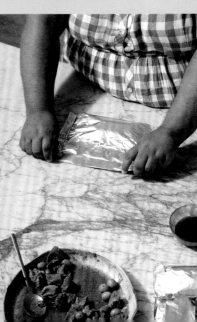

Spoon 2 tablespoons achiote oil on each foil square. Using the back of the spoon, spread the oil toward the edges of the square. Scoop 1 cup of the masa onto the achiote oil and form into a log in the middle of the square. From the carne guisada, place five pieces of the meat, four olives, and some braising liquid onto the masa. Feel free to add more filling if you want the pasteles packed with meat!

Take one end of the foil and bring it over to the other end, so both ends are touching; you now have a foil rectangle with masa in the middle. Give the top of the foil parcel three shallow folds, then do the same with the two sides. Go back to the top of the parcel and give one more good fold, partially covering the entire parcel. Fold in the sides until they meet the masa. Repeat to form the remaining pasteles. (At this point, you can freeze the packets for up to 1 year.)

Bring a large pot of salted water to a boil over high heat. Add the packets, foil and all, and boil for 45 minutes. (For frozen packets, take them directly from the freezer to the pot.) Open one packet and check to see if the masa and filling are cooked through and hot; the masa should be firm. If not, cook the remaining packets for another 15 minutes. When they're done, using tongs, transfer the parcels to a serving plate.

Carefully cut open the parcels, coax the pasteles out of their foil and onto the plate, and discard the foil. Enjoy.

Cooking whole hogs,
El Rancho de Apa, Guaynabo, Puerto Rico.

From Barbicu to Barbacoa

The word *barbacoa* first appeared in print in Gonzalo Fernández de Oviedo's 1526 account of his travels in the West Indies, *Historia General y Natural de las Indias*. The Tainos' open-fire cooking method was known as *barbicu*, but you know … the colonizers ain't got time to itemize. Hence, they called the whole damn operation—the cooking surface, technique, and food—*barbacoa*.

I'm not saying that the whole-hog method of the Carolinas was influenced by Puerto Rico. That would be wild to even consider. I am also not saying that the whole-hog method of cooking over an open fire exists only in the Carolinas and Puerto Rico. I am saying the vastly superior lechón of Puerto Rico should also get some attention in the discussion of barbecue.

It was in the early 1500s that the Spanish saw (and documented) Tainos cooking their food on a grid made of interwoven green wood over an open fire. The Spanish brought pigs to the southeast United States in that same century. Some historians have even said that as the Spanish explorers turned their expeditions north, they brought the cooking technique with them from the Caribbean. *Faulkner's County: The Historical Roots of Yoknapatawpha* asserts that when DeSoto and his Spanish soldiers arrived in December 1540, they barbecued a hog for the Chickasaw people. This might have been the first chronicling of a whole hog being cooked in the United States. The barbecue of the ancient Tainos might not look how you'd expect when you hear the word *barbecue*. But then, barbecue doesn't look like what most people expect, depending on where they live in this country. At the moment, I suspect most people think of barbecue as West Texas barbecue: fatty brisket and brontosaurus beef ribs. But, if you consider the whole-hog method in the Carolinas, where they cook the entire pig on a metal grate, over a bed of coals, why not consider lechón, the Puerto Rican method of spit-roasting a whole hog, low and slow, over sweltering coals.

Puerto Rican lechón has so many similarities to Carolina whole-hog barbecue, including the pepper-vinegar sauce of Eastern North Carolina, which is strikingly similar to Puerto Rico's pique. The Indigenous contribution often gets left out of the barbecue discussion despite the fact that Puerto Rico's ancestral tribe can be single-handedly credited for the word *barbicu*. Luckily, John T. Edge saw the similarities when he wrote about it in his essay for *Garden & Gun*, "Puerto Rican Pig Pickin'," and Seattle chef Eric Rivera has petitioned for lechón's place in national barbecue history.

Lechón

Makes 20 to 25 servings

This is admittedly the most involved recipe in this book, requiring two days of preparation and eight hours of cooking. Procuring a whole hog is not as difficult as you'd think. Most Asian stores provide this service, or you can ask the butcher at your local supermarket. I choose to source a whole hog through Rancho Llano Seco, the same local and sustainable sixth-generation family farm that I mentioned in my Chuletas recipe (see page 124). I could have gone the route of cooking the pig in a Caja China roasting box or using the butterflied, or splayed-open, method that many in the United States seem to use. But that's not how Puerto Ricans roast their pigs. My grandma taught my mom how to roast a pig over an open fire, and my mom taught me. I don't know nothing about roasting a whole hog with gas. I also build my fire directly on the ground, in the dirt. That's the only way that I can tell you how to build it. So, unless you have a patch of backyard that you don't mind burning up, I suggest you do your research on how to accomplish another option. I know how to roast a pig by sight and smell. Writing the vernacular is a whole other ball game. And there are tools that I've acquired that I apply in an unorthodox manner to achieve my goal, like using a carving fork to make holes where I can insert wire to wrap around the pig's spine and the pole. This ensures that the hog is more stable. One of the most important things about roasting a whole hog on a spit is to keep the pig moving. Keeping the pig moving means even heat distribution. For a list of materials you'll need to build a hog-roasting setup, check out page 141.

In Puerto Rico, the men roast the hog, and the women are left to figure out how to repurpose the innards and leftovers and transform them into tasty tidbits. While I was doing the research for whole-hog roasting to figure out the proportions, I read in a book (written by a woman) that roasting a whole hog is a man's job. Coming from a matriarchal family, we weren't lucky (or patient) enough to rely on a man if we wanted to roast a whole hog for someone's birthday. My nana was, like, "The shit needs to be done and we're the only ones to do it." And it's not as if any of us were celebrated for doing so!

continued ▶

Lechón, continued

1 (50-pound) whole pig
(see Note)

Juice from 2 large oranges

Juice from 2 medium lemons

1 head garlic, coarsely chopped

2 cups sofrito (see page 23)

2 cups table salt (see Note)

1 cup distilled white vinegar

1 cup dried oregano

¼ cup sazón (see page 19)

¼ cup garlic powder

2 cups achiote oil (see page 19)

Assemble all the materials listed on page 141. On the sanitized prep table, give the pig a real good wash, inside and out, with a backyard water hose. Like humans, a pig's dirty areas are the ears, snout, and feet. Make sure you scrub those hella good and then pat dry with paper towels.

In a large bowl, combine the orange juice, lemon juice, chopped garlic, sofrito, 1 cup of the salt, vinegar, ½ cup of the oregano, sazón, and garlic powder and stir to form a marinade. Rub the inside of the pig with about half of the marinade. Using the boning knife, stab numerous slits all over the pig. (This is Mami's method.) Now thoroughly rub the outside of the pig with the remaining marinade, then use your marinade-y wet hands to rub the remaining 1 cup salt and remaining ½ cup oregano on the outside of the pig. Make sure to get some of the seasoning in the slits and between the skin and the ribs; you can lift or separate the skin just as you would with a chicken. Use the boning knife if necessary.

Place the pig in one of the trash bags. Let marinate overnight in the fridge or in a large cooler with the ice. (Place each bag of ice inside a remaining trash bag; if the ice bag bursts open or leaks overnight, the water will remain inside the outer bags and not on the pig. (Please don't be that person that puts the pig in the bathtub.) Clean and sanitize the prep table.

When ready to build your roasting "pit," you will essentially create a rectangular open-oven by placing two or three of the concrete blocks, vertically, on the left side of a patch of bare dirt (away from any plants or grass) that extends the length of the pig and then another two or three concrete blocks, vertically, on the right side of that dirt. The area between the blocks, for the hot coals, should be a 4-foot gap. Top each side with two concrete blocks, lying them horizontally, on top of the vertical blocks. Add another two blocks, horizontally, behind your vertical blocks to reinforce them. If you like, add the remaining four concrete blocks, horizontally, two per side, to the outside walls for added structural integrity.

Using the screwdriver and wood screws, attach two caster wheels onto each 4 by 6-inch piece of scrap wood, leaving a 1½-inch gap between the wheels. Place one caster-wheel device, wheels up, on each concrete-block wall; this is gonna make turning your pig much easier. On the side of the pit farthest away from you, lay one of the corrugated roof panels on the outside of the blocks; it'll slightly lean forward.

About 45 minutes before you're ready to cook the pig, dump one of the bags of charcoal briquettes and half a bag of the lump charcoal directly into the pit. Add some twisted newspaper to help the fire catch, pour a conservative amount of lighter fluid onto the newspaper and charcoal, and set a lit match to it. (Or, you can use one of those charcoal chimneys.)

Mami stokes the fire.

Put the 8-foot pole into the anus of the pig and push it through until it comes out the pig's mouth. Align the pig's spine with the pole and, using the carving fork, poke holes along the pig's sides near the spine. Then, using the long-nose pliers, thread the stainless-steel wire through those holes and around the pig's spine and the pole; this will steady the pig. Wire the pig's legs to the pole and then pull the pig's cavity shut, piercing the skin with the end of the wire to "sew" it closed. (Alternatively, you can use a large meat-trussing needle and butcher's twine to close it.) Place the ends of the pole on the caster-wheel devices and then two people must continuously hand-rotate the pole (and if you've secured your pig, the pig will follow) throughout the cooking process.

continued ▶

David Santana helps prepare the pig for roasting.

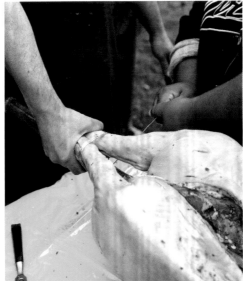

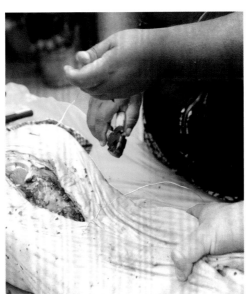

Lechón, continued

You will need to add about 10 pounds of charcoal (half lump, half briquettes) per hour of cooking time; the pig cooks for 6 to 8 hours. You gotta keep the fire hot. After the first 30 minutes of cooking time, using the pastry brush, paint the hog with some of the achiote oil. As the hog cooks, once every 30 minutes, paint the exterior with the remaining achiote oil. For the last 2 hours, remove a horizontal concrete block from each side, bringing the pig closer to the fire so that the skin on the butt and head has a chance to blister. Using the shovel, shift the hot charcoals from directly under the midsection of the pig to under the head and the butt. Only the head and butt should have coals under them now. Place the second roof panel on the other side of the pig. After 1 hour, place the meat thermometer in the thickest part of the pig—the thighs, legs, and ham. When the temperature registers 165°F, your hog is done. If it's not finished, leave for another hour and then check the temp again.

Top the clean prep table with the cutting boards. Everything is going to happen on your cutting boards. Lift the pig off the fire and transfer it to the prepared table; people will already be starting to gather around. Remove all the wires and the pole. With Puerto Ricans, the skin goes first. With the butcher knife, separate the skin from the meat, handing everyone a piece of skin. Then break down the pig by separating the head and hams (butt) from the midsection and placing on the baking sheets. Cut the hog in front of the hips and behind the shoulders. You may need to use the mallet to chop down with some force on some of the cuts; much in the same manner as the lechoneros in Puerto Rico. Finally, chop the meat into bite-size pieces before using the tongs to serve.

Notes: A pound of meat per person feels generous and yields enough for everyone to eat and take home leftovers. Here's how to gauge cooked weight and servings.

- **A 75-pound pig will give you about 30 pounds cooked pork and 30 to 35 servings**

- **A 100-pound pig will give you about 40 pounds cooked pork and 40 to 45 servings**

- **A 125-pound pig will give you about 50 pounds cooked pork and 50 to 55 servings**

You must use table salt because the granules are so fine that they dissolve evenly. If you choose to use the larger granules of kosher salt, just know they might not dissolve; this will create a salt crust.

If you decide to use a paintbrush, make sure it's brand-new and never been used. But you can then use it over and over for your future pigs or any other cooking.

Basting and roasting.

The finished product.

Hog Roast Materials

Before making your own lechón, first gather the materials that you'll need to prep it, roast it, and break it down after cooking:

- Sanitized table long enough to fit your whole hog—and random shit

- Boning knife

- 1 to 4 unscented 40-gallon trash bags

- Cooler large enough to fit your pig (optional)

- 3 (20-pound) bags ice (optional)

- 12 to 18 (8 by 8 by 16-inch) concrete blocks

- Screwdriver

- 8 (#2 x ¼-inch) wood screws

- 4 caster wheels with mounting plates and brakes

- 2 (4 by 6-inch) pieces scrap wood

- 2 (8-foot-long) corrugated galvanized-steel 29-gauge roof panels

- 3 (20-pound) bags charcoal briquettes

- 2 (17.6-pound) bags natural lump charcoal

- Newspaper, lighter fluid, and matches as needed

- 8-foot-long, 2-inch diameter bamboo pole

- Heavy-duty carving fork

- Long-nose pliers, with wire cutting tool (or a separate pair of wire cutters)

- 25 feet (55-pound, 16-gauge) stainless-steel wire

- Pastry brush or paintbrush (see Note, page 138)

- Shovel

- Meat thermometer

- Large cutting boards

- Super-sharp butcher knife or machete

- Large baking sheets

- Mallet

- Tongs

Beef

When I was a columnist for the *San Francisco Chronicle*, I wrote about the Chinese impact on Puerto Rico. Few people outside of the island know about this phenomenon. Even on an island, various cultures eventually affect gastronomic and genetic makeup. Much like the rest of the world, immigrants have come to Puerto Rico in search of a better life or occupation. As their contributions become ingrained in the everyday repertoire, some can also become economically critical.

The United States' canned meats stole the affections of Puerto Ricans when the population learned to "Creolize" products such as Spam and corned beef, adding tomato sauce and sofrito to make dishes that were more palatable to their tastes. Black beans arrived on the scene when an influx of Cubans fleeing the revolution came to Puerto Rico. As a result, moros y cristianos—black beans cooked in rice—spread across the island so much that most Puerto Ricans born after the 1960s consider black beans a traditional part of the Puerto Rican diet. The variety of pink beans of my grandmother's childhood are all but impossible to find today.

The Cuban revolution also brought an influx of Cuban Chinese immigrants. The earliest documented Chinese restaurant in Puerto Rico is Hing's Restaurant, which opened in 1951. The Puerto Rico tourism office got on board with helping to market Chinese restaurants because it was a great tourist attraction.

While the most widespread gastronomic contribution by Chinese immigrants to Puerto Rico might have been ice cream (see page 199), you can also find their mash-up creations: a Chinese takeout combo that comes with protein, fried rice, and your choice of french fries or tostones. Another is mofongo topped with black pepper steak.

Picadillo

Makes 4 servings

Picadillo is as versatile as hell. It's used to fill empanadas, alcapurrias, piñóns, pastelóns, or just served over rice with a side of maduros. I tend to use ground bison these days because I've read that it's more sustainable and slightly more healthful than using beef. It's also not hard to track down. Although I purchase mine at the local co-op, I've heard they also sell it at Walmart.

2 tablespoons olive oil

1 russet potato, coarsely diced

Kosher salt

Freshly ground black pepper

1 medium yellow onion, coarsely chopped

4 garlic cloves, coarsely minced

1 pound ground bison or ground beef

1 tablespoon sazón (see page 19)

2 teaspoons dried oregano

1 teaspoon ground cumin

1 cup tomato sauce

½ cup sofrito (see page 23)

2 tablespoons finely minced olives, plus 2 tablespoons olive brine

1 tablespoon finely minced capers

Basic White Rice (page 164) for serving

Add the olive oil to a skillet and place over medium-high heat. Add the potato, season with salt and pepper, and cook for 2 to 3 minutes. Add the onion and cook for 2 to 3 minutes more, or until soft. Add the garlic and cook for 1 to 2 minutes, or until translucent.

Add the bison to the skillet and season with the sazón, oregano, cumin, salt, and pepper. Mix to combine the meat and spices and then brown the meat for 3 minutes, breaking it apart with a wooden spoon as it cooks. Stir in the tomato sauce, sofrito, olives, and capers and cook the mixture down for 15 to 20 minutes. Stir in the olive brine and cook for 5 minutes more.

Serve the picadillo over rice.

Pepper Steak

Makes 4 servings

Normally made in searing hot woks, this is a quick-cooking dish. You are using wafer-thin slices of lean steak and cooking them over high heat. It can be served over rice or, for a true Chino-Boricua experience, serve it over mofongo.

1 pound flank steak, sliced ¼ inch thick

¼ teaspoon baking soda

5 tablespoons water, or as needed

2½ tablespoons cornstarch, or as needed

1 teaspoon canola oil, plus 2 tablespoons

2 teaspoons soy sauce, plus 2 tablespoons

1 cup coarsely chopped green bell pepper

½ cup coarsely chopped white onion

2 teaspoons All-Purpose Adobo (page 20)

1 teaspoon granulated sugar

½ teaspoon sesame oil

Mofongo (page 188), Arroz Chino Boricua (page 171), or Basic White Rice (page 164) for serving

Using a mallet, pound the flank steak pieces super-thin (about $1/16$ inch thick) to tenderize. You want to make sure the beef is as tender as possible. In a bowl large enough to hold the beef, whisk the baking soda into 3 tablespoons of the water. Add the beef and massage it with your hands until all the liquid has been absorbed. Mix in 1½ teaspoons of the cornstarch, the 1 teaspoon canola oil, and 2 teaspoons soy sauce and set aside to marinate for at least 15 minutes or up to 1 hour.

Bring a pot of water to boil over high heat.

Add the beef, bell pepper, and onion to the water and blanch 1 to 2 minutes, or until the color of the bell pepper brightens and the meat turns from pink to brown. Drain the meat and bell pepper and set aside.

In a small bowl, combine the adobo, sugar, sesame oil, remaining 2 tablespoons water, remaining 2 tablespoons cornstarch, and remaining 2 tablespoons soy sauce. Stir to mix and set aside.

Add the remaining 2 tablespoons canola oil to a cast-iron skillet and place over high heat. Add the beef and cook until crusty and browned, 5 to 7 minutes. Transfer the beef to a bowl and set aside.

Turn the heat to medium-high and add the sesame oil mixture to the skillet and keep stirring as it simmers and thickens. (If it's looking too thick, add a splash more water; if it's too thin, mix 1 teaspoon water and 2 teaspoons cornstarch into a slurry and stir into the skillet.) Add the beef, onion, and bell pepper and mix thoroughly with the sauce, ensuring everything is coated, and sauté for about 6 minutes.

Serve the pepper steak immediately with mofongo, arroz chino, or white rice.

Jibarito

Makes 4 servings

The jibarito was created in Chicago, making it a Diasporican creation! In the late 1990s, Juan "Peter" Figueroa and his brothers owned Borinquen Restaurant in the predominantly Puerto Rican community of Humboldt Park. Figueroa got the idea for this dish from a recipe in Puerto Rican newspaper *El Vocero* for a "sandwich de plátano," which used two big-ass tostones instead of bread. The recipe was from Plátano Loco, a restaurant in Puerto Rico that is still in operation. Figueroa gave his creation a recognizable folkloric name and started serving it in his restaurant, and soon the sandwich's popularity could not be contained. Now there's even a jibarito for which amarillos are used in place of tostones. Borinquen Restaurant has since closed (but Juan's brother Angel's location, Borinquen Lounge, is open and serves the jibarito), and many restaurants have since taken the idea for their own profit without credit to Figueroa.

You can dress the plátanos with a simple garlic-parsley butter sauce instead of or in addition to the mayoketchup. (I never have the patience to make the mayoketchup when I'm making this sandwich for just myself.)

2 tablespoons olive oil

2 large onions, julienned ¼ inch thick

5 garlic cloves

3 cups water

2 tablespoons sazón (see page 19)

2 tablespoons All-Purpose Adobo (page 20)

2 tablespoons distilled white vinegar

2 rib-eye round steaks, sliced super-thinly

Canola oil for frying

4 plátanos, peeled (see page 12) and sliced in half lengthwise; holding water seasoned with garlic powder

Kosher salt

Mayoketchup (see page 20) for slathering

Whole lettuce leaves of your choosing, well washed, for topping

2 heirloom tomatoes, sliced

4 slices American cheese

1 teaspoon garlic spread (such as Lawrys; optional)

Add the olive oil to a pot over medium-high heat. Add the onions and garlic cloves and sauté for about 3 minutes. Stir in the water, sazón, adobo, and vinegar; turn the heat to low; and bring to a simmer. Add the steaks and let simmer for 20 to 30 minutes, or until the beef is tender. Set aside.

Fill a 10-inch cast-iron skillet with 2 inches of canola oil and place over medium-high heat. You want enough oil to cover the plátanos. Heat the oil until it registers 350°F on an instant-read thermometer. (Add a tiny piece of plátano; if the oil sizzles, it's ready for frying.) Add the plátanos in batches and fry for 5 to 8 minutes, or until fork-soft. Set them aside and turn off the heat.

Using a large plate, cast-iron skillet, baking sheet, large tortilla press, or cutting board (anything big enough to cover the plátanos), press down extremely hard on the plátano halves to flatten them. They must be as flat and wide as you can get them. This takes some finagling, because you might have to wiggle the plate (or whatever flattened surface you're crushing them with) while *also* pressing down. Scoop the flattened plantains off the surface with a spatula.

continued ▶

Line a plate with paper towels and place near the stove. Bring the oil back to 350°F over medium-high heat. Add the plátanos again in batches and fry, this time for 3 to 5 minutes, or until crispy. Using tongs, transfer the plátanos to the prepared plate. Season with salt.

Just as you would a piece of bread for a sandwich, slather one side of each plátano with mayoketchup. Top four of the plátanos with the lettuce, tomatoes, cheese, beef, and onions from the braising liquid; let some of the juices come along with the meat. Cap with another plátano, mayoketchup-side down. Cut the sandwiches in half, horizontally, top with the garlic spread, if desired, and serve immediately.

Braised Corned Beef

Makes 4 servings

Yeah, that's right. Much like Spam makes an appearance in the form of a guisada, canned corned beef has also been Creolized for Puerto Rican taste buds. I don't make mine in the traditional way because I find it's usually a bit on the soupy side for me. I add texture by using corned beef hash and caramelizing the hell out of the mixture before adding the sofrito and tomato sauce.

2 tablespoons canola oil

1 (15-ounce) can corned beef hash

½ cup sofrito (see page 23)

¼ cup tomato sauce

1 tablespoon sazón (see page 19)

Kosher salt

Freshly ground black pepper

½ to 1 cup water

Basic White Rice (page 164) for serving

Add the canola oil to a 10-inch cast-iron skillet and place over medium-high heat. Add the corned beef hash and sauté for 5 to 7 minutes, flipping it while trying not to break it up too much, until a sizable crust forms.

Add the sofrito, tomato sauce, and sazón and season with salt and pepper. Add enough of the water to loosen the mixture to your desired consistency, then turn the heat to low and let simmer for 15 minutes.

Serve the corned beef over rice.

Carne Guisada

Makes 4 to 6 servings

I make this dish all the time and, yet, I never tire of it. Sometimes I use pork, sometimes I use chicken, and very infrequently I use beef. The beef version is the most delicious, in my opinion, but it's also the richest. I use the same cut of beef for when I make pot roast or beef stew; it's a tender cut that has a decent amount of fat. If you cut it into small chunks, it cooks quickly and tenderly. This could easily become a part of your regular weeknight meal rotation.

2 tablespoons canola oil or vegetable oil

1½ pounds boneless chuck roast, cut into 1-inch chunks

1 medium yellow onion, chopped

2 cups water, or as needed

½ cup tomato sauce

½ cup unpitted Manzanilla green olives (optional)

1 large russet potato, peeled and diced

¼ cup sofrito (see page 23)

1 tablespoon sazón (see page 19)

Kosher salt

Freshly ground black pepper

Basic White Rice (page 164) for serving

Add the canola oil to a large heavy-bottomed pot and place over medium-high heat. Add the chuck roast and sear for 3 to 5 minutes, or until golden brown. Add the onion and cook for 2 to 3 minutes, or until translucent. Stir in the water, tomato sauce, half of the olives and potato pieces, 2 tablespoons of the sofrito, and the sazón, then scrape the bottom of the pot with a wooden spoon to loosen all the brown bits. Turn the heat to low and let simmer, partially covered, for 1 hour, keeping an eye on it because the potato will thicken the broth and you might need to add more water.

Add the remaining half of the potato to the pot, season with salt and pepper, and cook for 15 to 20 minutes, or until the potato pieces are fork-tender. Add the remaining 2 tablespoons sofrito and remaining olives and stir to distribute well.

Serve the guisada over rice.

Puerto Rican Meat Logs

Makes 4 to 6 servings

I can't remember how or when I came up with these little meat rockets. To me, it's just another Diasporican recipe. It was probably one of those weekdays when I had some ground bison and a cabinet full of spices and cans of tomato sauce. That describes my pantry in a nutshell. Ras el hanout is a North African spice blend—much like adobo or sazón, everyone has their own special blend—with a base containing cinnamon, cloves, paprika, and fenugreek. This dish is extremely warming and floral. Braise the meat logs in a sofrito-laced tomato sauce and spoon over rice or couscous.

¼ cup olive oil

1 large yellow onion, coarsely chopped

5 garlic cloves, coarsely chopped

1 pound ground bison or ground beef

Kosher salt

Freshly ground black pepper

2 tablespoons ras el hanout

2 tablespoons Illyanna's Adobo (page 20)

2 tablespoons granulated garlic

1 tablespoon ground turmeric

1 tablespoon sazón (see page 19)

1 cup sofrito (see page 23)

1 cup bread crumbs

½ cup water, chicken stock, or vegetable stock

1 (8-ounce) can tomato sauce

1 bunch red chard, leaves stripped from stems and finely chopped

4 cups cooked couscous or white rice (see page 164)

Chopped parsley for garnishing (optional)

Add 2 tablespoons of the olive oil to a large skillet and place over medium-high heat. Add the onion and sauté 2 to 4 minutes, or until translucent. Then add the garlic and sauté 1 to 2 minutes more. Transfer the onion and garlic to a small bowl and set aside to cool. Turn off the heat.

Put the bison in a bowl and season with salt, pepper, the ras el hanout, adobo, granulated garlic, turmeric, sazón, and ½ cup of the sofrito. Add half of the cooled onion-garlic mixture and all the bread crumbs and use your hands to mix until all the ingredients are thoroughly combined. Shape the meat mixture into as many elongated logs (or mini meatloaves) as you can get—about a dozen 4-inch logs.

Place the skillet, without wiping it out, over medium-high heat. Add the remaining 2 tablespoons olive oil and a few of the meat logs and sear on all sides for 3 to 5 minutes total, or until crusty and brown. Transfer the logs to a plate and repeat to make the remaining ones. Set aside.

Add the water, tomato sauce, remaining onion-garlic mixture, and remaining ½ cup sofrito to the skillet and stir to combine. Stir in the chard, turn the heat to low, and let simmer in the sauce for 6 to 8 minutes, or until tender. Return the meat logs to the skillet and let simmer in the sauce for 10 to 15 minutes, or until they are cooked to your desired doneness (pierce one with a knife tip to test) and the sauce has thickened.

Serve the meat logs, sauce, and greens over couscous or rice, garnished with parsley, if desired.

Bistec Encebollado

Makes 4 servings

Nana used to make this dish with liver for me when I was a kid. When it's made with liver, it's called higado encebollado. I'd slip the liver and onions between two pieces of white Wonder Bread slathered with mayonnaise. You don't have to marinate your steaks overnight. This is still a delicious dish if you marinate them for just 10 minutes while you prep the onion. The overnight marinade is mostly for those who have access only to supermarket cube steaks, which tend to be on the tougher side.

4 cube steaks (about 1¼ pounds total)

Kosher salt

Freshly ground black pepper

2 garlic cloves

½ cup distilled white vinegar

3 tablespoons olive oil

2 tablespoons soy sauce

2 tablespoons granulated garlic

¼ cup canola oil, or as needed

2 medium yellow onions, thinly sliced into rings

2 cups water

Basic White Rice (page 164) for serving

Although cube steaks are already tenderized, I find that some supermarkets sometimes don't do a good job of this. So, place the steaks on a cutting board and using the "tooth" part of a meat mallet, pound the steaks five times per piece. Season the steaks with salt and pepper. In a pilón or other mortar and pestle, mash the garlic cloves. Add the vinegar, olive oil, 1 tablespoon of the soy sauce, and granulated garlic to the pilón and combine with the mashed garlic. Transfer this marinade to a bowl or container large enough to hold the steaks snugly. Add the steaks to the marinade and let marinate in the refrigerator for up to 24 hours.

Add the canola oil to a 12-inch cast-iron skillet and place over medium heat. Remove the steaks from the marinade and pat dry with paper towels; reserve the marinade. Add two of the steaks to the oil and fry for 5 to 7 minutes, or until cooked to your liking. Repeat with the remaining steaks, adding oil as needed, and then set aside.

Add half of the onion rings and another 1 tablespoon canola oil, if necessary, to the pan drippings and cook for 2 to 3 minutes, or until translucent. Stir in the reserved marinade, water, and remaining 1 tablespoon soy sauce and braise for about 25 minutes. Add the remaining onion rings and cook for 5 minutes more; the sauce should have reduced and almost entirely evaporated.

Serve the steaks and the juice over white rice, spooning the remaining sauce over everything.

Piñón

Makes 6 servings

Here's another "whodunnit" scenario. In my opinion, pastelón, piñón, canoa, and piononos are quadruplets that attempt to present themselves differently to create their own identities and be recognized. Depending on which part of the island you're on and to whom you're talking, some of these can be considered the same dish . . . or the other one. Following me?

The pastelón is usually made with mashed amarillos, whereas piñóns are made with strips of amarillos and green beans, both of which are built up like a lasagna. Piononos are long strips of amarillo that encase a filling and then those pucks are deep-fried. Canoas are fried whole amarillos that are then slit down the middle, stuffed with picadillo, topped with cheese, and roasted until the cheese is bubbling and browned. They are for those who are, like, *fuck this shit*, and pile all the fillings on top of a amarillo and throw it into the oven. All four have the same—the same!—flavor profile. Don't let anyone try and gaslight you into thinking they taste different. They don't. However, they all *look* different. And the piñón is by far the most chulo of them all.

Canola oil for frying

5 ripe amarillos, peeled (see "Peeling Guineos and Plátanos," page 12) and sliced thinly lengthwise

1 pound ground bison or ground beef

1 cup tomato sauce

½ cup sofrito (see page 23)

1 tablespoon All-Purpose Adobo (page 20)

1 tablespoon sazón (see page 19)

Olive brine for sprinkling

2 cups shredded mozzarella cheese

1 egg, whisked

Basic White Rice (page 164) for serving (optional)

Preheat the oven to 350°F.

Line a plate with paper towels and set near the stove. Fill a 12-inch cast-iron skillet with 1 inch of canola oil and place over medium-high heat. You want enough oil to partially submerge the amarillos. Heat the oil until it registers 350°F on an instant-read thermometer. (Add a tiny piece of amarillo to the oil; if the oil sizzles, it's ready for frying.)

Add the amarillo slices, in batches, to the oil and fry for 5 to 7 minutes, using tongs to flip them as they fry, or until browned and tender. Transfer the slices to the prepared plate. Repeat to cook the remaining slices. Discard the oil.

In the same pan, without wiping it out, over medium-high heat, add the bison and sauté for 2 to 3 minutes. Stir in the tomato sauce, sofrito, adobo, and sazón; turn the heat to low; and let simmer for about 15 minutes.

In a 9 by 9-inch pan, place the amarillo slices in a single layer, ensuring they slightly overlap. Spoon the bison mixture on top of the amarillo slices and sprinkle with olive brine. Add a layer of cheese. Repeat the process until you run out of room in the pan or amarillos. Pour the egg evenly over the amarillos. Sprinkle with the cheese; making sure it is on top of the final layer.

Bake for 30 to 40 minutes. If your cheese isn't browned and bubbly, crank up the heat or turn on the broiler for the last minute or two. Let the piñón cool for about 10 minutes so that its layers can form and set. (It'll be prettier when you cut it if you let it cool. But Mami and I never wait for our food to cool down.)

Serve the piñón by itself or with a side of white rice.

Spaghetti with Not Fideos

Makes 6 to 8 servings

When Nana used to make spaghetti, like most of her food, she'd use an obscene amount of oil. So greasy. And having never seen pasta before, she'd use fideos. With canned pasta sauce (Ragú) not readily available at local bodegas, Nana made her sauce as close to her neighbor Maria's pasta sauce as she could. But, you know, with Puerto Rican flair. Tomato sauce? Got that. Garlic? Why not super-garlicky adobo? Ooh, sazón for color. To the naked eye, Nana's spaghetti looks like any ordinary spaghetti. But, as soon as the sauce touches the tip of your tongue, the adobo and sazón blast your brain, leaving your eyebrows suspended at the top of your forehead like a chola who's surprised. I don't like any of that! I don't appreciate the texture of fideos in spaghetti and meat sauce; their weight sort of turns into a clumpy mound. Instead, I use regular spaghetti noodles and Mami's spaghetti sauce recipe, which you also might find just as unorthodox. What's so unorthodox about it? Well, she doctors up canned sauce with a spaghetti seasoning packet and adds Hillshire Farm smoked sausage.

2 tablespoons olive oil

1 large yellow onion, coarsely diced

7 garlic cloves, coarsely diced

6 ounces Hillshire Farm smoked sausage, cut into ¼-inch-thick slices

1 pound ground bison or ground beef

1 packet spaghetti sauce seasoning

3 ounces tomato paste

4 ounces tomato sauce

4 to 6 cups water

Kosher salt

Freshly ground black pepper

1 tablespoon granulated sugar (optional)

1 pound dried spaghetti

Add the olive oil to a stockpot and place over medium-high heat. Add the onion and sauté for 3 to 4 minutes, or until softened, then add the garlic and sauté for 1 to 2 minutes more. Add the sausage and brown well for 2 to 4 minutes, then add the bison, breaking the meat apart with a wooden spoon, and cook for 3 minutes. Add the spaghetti sauce seasoning and stir to combine well, then add the tomato paste and stir again. Then stir in the tomato sauce and 4 cups of the water and season with salt and pepper. You want the flavors of the tomato paste and sauce to develop and caramelize, so they're less acidic. Turn the heat to medium and let simmer for 30 to 40 minutes, adding more of the water as needed for your desired consistency. Taste and add the sugar, if necessary.

Bring a separate pot of salted water to a boil over high heat. Add the spaghetti and cook to your desired texture. Drain the spaghetti, add to the sauce, stir to combine well, and cook for 1 minute.

Serve the spaghetti immediately.

Sloppy Joes

Makes 4 to 6 servings

Mami would often make open-face sloppy joes. There were only a few times she used the Manwich brand, preferring her own homemade blend of seasonings instead. She'd also add a can of Van Camp's pork and beans. I decided to remake my childhood classic, hyping the flavor up to 11 but keeping the can of pork and beans in the mix. We only ever had Wonder Bread in our household; choose whatever white bread you're nostalgic for.

2 tablespoons olive oil

1 large yellow onion, coarsely diced

5 garlic cloves, coarsely diced

1 pound ground bison or ground beef

1 (15-ounce) can pork and beans (preferably Van Camp's)

1 (8-ounce) can tomato sauce

¼ cup sofrito (see page 23)

2 tablespoons Illyanna's Adobo (page 20)

2 tablespoons light brown sugar

2 tablespoons fish sauce

1 tablespoon soy sauce

1 to 2 cups water

Sriracha for seasoning

Kosher salt

Freshly ground black pepper

8 to 10 slices toasted soft white bread, or hamburger buns

Add the olive oil to a stockpot and place over medium-high heat. Add the onion and sauté for 3 to 4 minutes, or until softened, then add the garlic and sauté for 1 to 2 minutes more. Add the bison and cook for 3 minutes, breaking the meat apart with a wooden spoon. Stir in the pork and beans, tomato sauce, sofrito, adobo, brown sugar, fish sauce, soy sauce, and enough of the water to make a loose mixture. Season with sriracha, salt, and pepper. Turn the heat to medium and let simmer for 30 to 40 minutes, or until the sauce has thickened.

Serve the sloppy joes over or sandwiched between the bread.

Rice and Other Grains

Rice was brought to the island by the Spanish in the very early days of their conquest. The Spanish thought the Taino would know how to handle rice crops because they were successful in cultivating maize. The Taino didn't. It wasn't until enslaved Africans were brought to the island to work the sugarcane plantations that rice crops began to flourish because the Africans had already cultivated and eaten rice in their homelands long before the Spanish conquest of the Americas. This led to an infinite number of rice dishes in Puerto Rico—con patitas, con jueyes, con habichuelas, con gandules, con pollo, con coco, arroz pasteles, rice pudding, rice fritters, rice cheeseballs. The chosen variety was medium-grain rice.

Because Puerto Rican food is a soldering of genetic strains from various continents, violence had to happen for the cuisine to exist as we know it today. Arroz con gandules is made with sofrito, rice, pork, and pigeon peas. The recao in the sofrito is from the Taino, the pork from Spain, and the pigeon peas from Africa. So, violence has always been present in my culture. It appears in the shadows, on the backs of those fighting for independence, written in calligraphy on a leather belt that hangs from a rusty nail in a living room, and in the streets of underrepresented socioeconomic communities. From the decimation of most of our Taino ancestors to the loss of more than four thousand of our gente in the aftermath of Hurricane Maria, violence is always there. I have known violence all my life too. It was the soundtrack to my childhood. It's the place that I immediately go to when I am frustrated or feel I have been bamboozled.

Opposite, inset: Arroz con jueyes, Millie's Restaurant, Toa Alta, Puerto Rico.

There are vivid moments in my memory bank when I recall questioning if violence was normal. Growing up in Sacramento, we lived in a one-bedroom wooden casita with a detached garage on a corner parcel of land that had two other houses enclosed by a single fence. The houses made a billiards-cue triangle shape. An abandoned L-shaped field gave a one-armed hug to our occupied land. I commonly refer to it as "the compound." I don't recollect my mother ever letting me or my visiting cousins off the compound. We had more than enough room to ride our bikes within the confines of the long chain-link fence. There was an apple tree, a plum tree, a mighty magnolia, and blackberry brambles. Mrs. Brown, our landlady, lived in the largest house and our neighbor Marianne lived in the small house in the corner. I remember one summer day—it seemed like it was always summer—particularly well when I was about to start kindergarten. I was outside jumping off a metal barstool–turned–diving board when I had to go to the bathroom. I ran through the kitchen, made a sharp left into my bedroom, quickly stole a glance at my mom, and walked through to the bathroom. I didn't entirely comprehend what was happening when I looked at my mother, but I had taken enough notice that the image remains vivid: My mother was helplessly on her back, eyes grotesquely bulging, gasping for air, with Vicente's hands firmly around her neck.

Vicente was Marianne's brother. Vicente and Marianne were extremely good-looking, both born of Portuguese parents. Vicente had thick jet-black hair, a thick black mustache, skin the color of redwood trees, and a manipulative smile. Marianne looked like Teena Marie, the singer. Vicente and Marianne were also completely unpredictable, having suffered their own traumas. It was the first time that I had seen domestic violence. Until then, it usually came in the form of muffled sounds behind closed doors. I queried my nana to explain what I had seen. Nana stopped frying the meat in the pot but never looked up at me. After a moment, she continued frying the meat but never answered me. She stood at the stove and dropped the sofrito into the hot oil until it sizzled and danced. She silently rushed cold water over medium-grain rice, swirling the bowl, using her hand as a sieve as she emptied the water into her hand and caught any wayward grains. She poured the rice into the sofrito and hot achiote oil, followed by tomato sauce, sazón, gandules, Manzanilla olives, and, a touch of her secret ingredient, olive brine. She swirled the mixture with her enamel spoon and covered it with a lid. Then we sat on her porch—I sat partially in the door frame with my bare legs on the concrete, and she sat in her plastic chair.

I silently watched the neighborhood "Bébé's Kids" running amok in their Airwalks, wearing their dookie gold chains, Jheri curls, and Locs. My nana embroidered a doily with a robin-in-flight pattern, purchased at Ben Franklin.

"Stir the rice, mija," she said suddenly. I ran into the kitchen and lifted the lid of her bare aluminum caldero, a blast of steam releasing. And with her spotted enamel cooking spoon, I shifted the rice from just above the base level to the top, being careful not to disturb it at the very bottom of the pot, just as she had shown me numerous times. It was the way to ensure the formation of the pegao—the celebrated crunchy burnt-rice layer. I put the lid back on the pot and returned to my spot on the porch.

Eternity went by before my grandma finally said, "Let's eat." I sat down at her kitchen table, which was covered by a white embroidered tablecloth covered by a large see-through plastic cover. She scooped hefty spoonfuls of the fluffy orange rice into a bowl and then, with elbow grease, scraped the bottom of the pot to excavate the pegao, placing the crunchy bits on top of the feathery rice. She placed the bowl of steaming arroz con gandules with large chunks of tender braised pork shoulder in front of me and then picked up the telephone receiver. "Papo?" she said. I ignored the rest like any well-trained kid did in those days. Food was present, so nothing else existed. I silently dug into my bowl of arroz con gandules and happily chomped away, savoring the rich pork, brightness from the olive brine, musk from the achiote, and floral from the recao, each rice grain separated and yet coagulated and finished off with the crunchiness of the pegao while fingering the pinto bean left on the photo of a sandia on my lotería card.

After that day, my uncle Papo came around to the compound more than ever. He spent entire days working on my mom's car, which had always seemed to run just fine whenever we'd use it on an errand. One day, I was holding the water hose for him while he washed his hands with Ajax, attempting to scrub away the dirt and oil that had caked in the lines on his palms. Looking straight past me, his eyes suddenly became fiery and fixed. When I turned around, I laid eyes on Vicente walking up the next-door driveway. "Can you get me a towel, mija?" Uncle Papo said. I ran inside and looked for car rags, but by the time I came back, Papo was gone. I never saw Vicente after that. And it was several months until I saw my uncle Papo again.

In my memories, I still see Vicente's menacing smile and what he did to my mom. I keep asking myself, though, *Why didn't I do anything in that immediate moment?*

Basic White Rice

Makes 6 servings

White rice is never *just* white rice when it comes to Puerto Rican food. It doesn't always accompany a dish but rather is its costar. Some Puerto Ricans often feel as though a meal isn't complete unless there's rice. When times were hard, which was often for many, rice was the only thing some people had to eat. And that meant ensuring that it tasted as delicious as possible by adding salt and fat. I don't add as much oil as my grandma did, but you can definitely taste the flavor of the oil and see how it coats the individual grains. In this recipe, I use Koda Farms rice since I love using local products as much as I can. And I also find their rice to be one of the more superior local brands that is similar to the medium-grain rice that my grandma used when I was a kid. I just use the measurements from the back of their Kokuho Rose rice package. And, honestly, you should be following the measurements on the back of all the rice packages.

⅓ cup canola oil or olive oil

1½ cups medium-grain rice, washed (see page 11)

2 cups water

Kosher salt

Add the canola oil to a medium caldero, or a wide and shallow stainless-steel pot, and place over medium-high heat. Add the rice and toast for 30 seconds.

Stir the water and 1 teaspoon salt into the rice; taste the liquid and add more salt as needed. Bring to a boil, uncovered, and allow the water to evaporate. Turn the heat to low, cover, and let simmer for 20 to 25 minutes, or until all the water has been absorbed and the grains of rice are tender.

Uncover the rice, turning it from the bottom to the top. If it is still wet, cover and cook for 5 to 10 minutes more, or until all the liquid has been absorbed and the rice is tender.

Fluff the rice with a fork and then serve.

Preserving the Taste of Memory

Koda Farms is the oldest continuously family-owned-and-operated rice farm and mill in California. Since the turn of the twentieth century, the Koda family has planted their heirloom rice in the San Joaquin Valley. Three generations later, Ross and Robin Koda, grandchildren of founder Keisaburo Koda, manage the farm. Kokuho Rose is a labor of love; compared to modern-day standards, this strain of rice is considered impractical to grow because it has a low yield and takes longer to mature than other varieties. The decision to continue to grow this style is their commitment to remember the past and a time when their family and hundreds of thousands of other Japanese and Japanese American families were sent to internment camps during World War II. And to remember that they persevered in the face of adversity, displacement, and racism.

Arroz con Gandules

Makes 4 to 6 servings

Some people would say that mofongo (see page 188) is Puerto Rico's national dish. Cue the "wrong" buzzer sound. Arroz con gandules (aka ACG) is the national dish. It's an extraordinary example of the island's history, encompassing ingredients that wouldn't exist without ancestors and conquerors. Pigeon peas can grow in poor soil and are drought-tolerant. They're also a shrub that likes the heat. And once entrenched, they will self-sow. ACG is a compound rice dish for which many different ingredients were added to the pot in an attempt to stretch it. Author Cruz Miguel Ortíz Cuadra stated in his book *Eating Puerto Rico* that arroz con gandules came together as a celebration dish because the gandules harvest coincides with Easter. My own belief is that people could harvest, sun-dry, and rehydrate the gandules at a later date, so the timing of their harvest has less to do with their importance to this dish than with their availability and versatility.

1 (15-ounce) can gandules

1 cup water

½ cup sofrito (see page 23)

¼ cup tomato sauce

¼ cup Manzanilla olives, with pits

1 tablespoon sazón (see page 19)

2 tablespoons canola oil

1 pound boneless pork shoulder ribs (also labeled as "country ribs"), diced into 1-inch chunks

1 cup long-grain rice, washed (see page 11)

Kosher salt

Freshly ground black pepper

In a large mixing bowl, combine the gandules, water, sofrito, tomato sauce, olives, and sazón and stir to incorporate. Set aside.

Add the canola oil to a large pot or deep pan and place over medium heat. Add the pork ribs and sear for 5 to 6 minutes, or until crispy and brown. Add the rice and stir for about 30 seconds to mix and brown. Add the sofrito mixture and stir to mix, then season with salt and pepper. Turn the heat to medium-high and bring to a boil.

Turn the heat to medium-low and cover—you don't want the heat too high, but you do want it hot enough to form the pegao (crust) at the bottom of the pot—and let simmer for 25 to 40 minutes, or until the rice is cooked through and the meat is tender. If your rice isn't fully cooked, fold the rice from near the bottom to the top, replace the lid, and cook for 10 minutes more, or until all the liquid has been absorbed and the rice is tender.

Fluff the rice with a fork and then serve immediately from the pot.

Note: When it comes to the amount of liquid you're adding (water, sofrito, tomato sauce, olive brine), consider what type of rice you're using. All your liquids should total the amount of "water" that your brand or variety of rice says to use on the back of its packaging. If the packaging says to use 1½ cups of water, that could mean 1 cup water, ¼ cup sofrito, and ¼ cup tomato sauce. It's one of the things that my nana forgot to tell me until I sat down and *watched* her make this dish. Sometimes she would do a combination of ¾ cup water, ¼ cup olive brine, ¼ cup sofrito, and ¼ cup tomato sauce.

Arroz con Jueyes

Makes 6 to 8 servings

The first time I had eaten arroz con jueyes was at El Burén de Lula in Loíza in 2015. While I was ordering everything on the menu, I asked if they had arroz con gandules to accompany the entrées, and the owner, and mystic, Maria Dolores de Jesus, known as "Lula," replied, "No. Because we make arroz con jueyes around here." Arroz con jueyes is not a dish that's in every Puerto Rican's repertoire. And it's not usually available year-round because it includes crab, and the crabs are seasonal. This dish is fundamentally a coastal specialty, as is Lula's cooking. Both arroz con gandules and arroz con jueyes are examples of how Puerto Rican cuisine has its regional dishes.

The Dungeness crab legs cook in their shells in this recipe.

1 cup water

½ cup sofrito (see page 23)

¼ cup tomato sauce

3 teaspoons sazón (see page 19)

2 tablespoons canola oil

1 cup long-grain rice, washed (see page 11)

Kosher salt

1 to 2 pounds Dungeness crab leg clusters

2 pounds Dungeness lump crabmeat

In a large mixing bowl, combine the water, sofrito, tomato sauce, and sazón and stir to incorporate. Set aside.

Add the canola oil to a large pot or deep pan and place over medium heat. Add the rice and stir to coat the grains, about 30 seconds. Add the sofrito mixture and stir to combine well, then season with salt. Turn the heat to medium-high and bring to a boil, then add the crab leg clusters, breaking some of the legs apart, and submerge in the liquid.

Turn the heat to medium-low and cover—you don't want the heat too high, but you do want it hot enough to form the pegao (crust) at the bottom of the pot—and let simmer for 20 minutes. Check to see if the rice is cooked through, then add the lump crabmeat and fold into the rice until evenly dispersed. Cover and cook for 5 to 10 minutes more. If your rice isn't fully cooked, fold the rice from near the bottom to the top, replace the lid, and cook for a few minutes more, or until all the liquid has been absorbed and the rice is tender.

Fluff the rice mixture with a fork and serve immediately, letting diners crack the crab legs and pick out the meat.

Arroz con Longaniza

Makes 6 to 8 servings

When you're buying longaniza for this recipe, you're not buying the Filipino kind (although I wouldn't be mad at someone who used the unsweetened longaniza de recado in a pinch). The evolution of the Spanish-style longaniza sausage was left to the devices of most of the Spanish colonies and morphed into various forms. Artisanal longaniza eateries can be found along La Ruta de la Longaniza that goes through Caguas, Orocovis, Morovis, and Naranjito in Puerto Rico. Naranjito is where Puerto Rico's famous restaurant El Rancho de Don Nando stands.

1 cup water

½ cup sofrito (see page 23)

¼ cup tomato sauce

1 tablespoon All-Purpose Adobo (page 20)

1 tablespoon sazón (see page 19)

1 teaspoon dried oregano

1 teaspoon ground cumin

1 tablespoon olive oil

1 pound longaniza, cut into large chunks

1 cup long-grain rice, washed (see page 11)

Kosher salt

Freshly ground black pepper

In a large mixing bowl, combine the water, sofrito, tomato sauce, adobo, sazón, oregano, and cumin and stir to incorporate. Set aside.

Add the olive oil to a large pot and place over medium heat. (A lot of fat will be released from the sausage, so you need just a little oil.) Add the longaniza and sear for 2 to 3 minutes. Add the rice and stir for about 30 seconds to mix and brown. Add the sofrito mixture and stir to combine well. Season with salt and pepper, then turn the heat to medium-high and bring to a boil.

Turn the heat to medium-low and cover—you don't want the heat too high, but you do want it hot enough to form the pegao (crust) at the bottom of the pot—and let simmer for 20 to 30 minutes. Check to see if the rice is cooked. If not, fold the rice from near the bottom to the top, replace the lid, and cook for 10 minutes more, or until all the liquid has been absorbed and the rice is tender.

Fluff the rice with a fork and then serve.

Note: You can buy longaniza online from Alcor Foods.

Arroz Chino Boricua

Makes 4 servings

If you read my column, you know about the impact, especially gastronomically, that the Chinese have had on Puerto Ricans. When you go into a Chinese restaurant in Puerto Rico and order a seemingly innocuous combo plate, what you receive might baffle a Statesider: an entrée, fried rice, and french fries or tostones. Yes, Chinese cooks have figured out Puerto Ricans' love affair with double starch and meat. You can also add peas and carrots to this mixture.

1 tablespoon canola oil

1 small yellow onion, diced

1 cup chopped jamonilla (such as Spam)

1 pound 16/20-count shrimp, peeled and deveined

2 scallions, chopped

2 teaspoons sofrito (see page 23)

2 eggs, beaten

2 cups Basic White Rice (page 164)

¼ cup soy sauce

Add the canola oil to a sauté pan and place over medium heat. Add the onion and cook for 2 to 3 minutes, or until translucent. Add the jamonilla and sauté for 2 to 3 minutes, or until browned, then stir to mix well.

Add the shrimp to the pan and sauté for 1 to 2 minutes, or until just pink, then add the scallions and sofrito and mix to combine. Add the eggs, let settle for 1 minute, and then scramble them in the pan for about 3 minutes. Add the rice, stir in the soy sauce, and keep the mixture moving for 5 to 7 minutes, or until the shrimp are thoroughly cooked.

Serve the rice hot.

Arroz Mamposteao

Makes 2 to 4 servings

Pronounced "mom-post-yeow," this rice dish calls for the week's leftovers—rice, beans, protein—combined in one pot. You can use any of Puerto Ricans' favored beans (pink, pinto, or kidney). You can also use any meat you have. You can add fresh onion and garlic in addition to your sofrito. You can even add fresh sweet or bell peppers! If you want a wetter rice (I do not like wet rice), you can add a little water or chicken stock. I've seen recipes that use ground beef or, more commonly, bacon. I remember my nana adding salt pork to hers. And so . . . I'm going old-school here.

1 cup medium-diced cured salt pork

2 tablespoons achiote oil (see page 19)

¼ cup sofrito (see page 23)

1 (15-ounce) can beans (see recipe introduction), drained

2 cups Basic White Rice (page 164)

Fill a saucepan halfway with water and place over medium-low heat. Bring to a simmer and add the salt pork. Blanch for 10 to 15 minutes, then drain and, using paper towels, pat the pork dry. Set aside.

Add the achiote oil to a medium pot and place over medium-high heat. Add the salt pork and render the fat for 5 to 8 minutes, or until browned and crispy. Pour off the fat, leaving 1 to 2 tablespoons in the pot. Add the sofrito and stir to distribute. Stir in the beans and rice and cover, letting the mixture meld and the bottom crisp for 10 to 15 minutes. Keep an eye on the rice so it doesn't blacken-burn on the bottom, adding just enough water to moisten the rice but not so much that it becomes mushy.

Serve the rice hot.

Casabe

Makes 4 servings

I'd like to think that Puerto Ricans love bread just as much as they love rice. In the mornings, bread is eaten with cheese and coffee for a light breakfast. In the afternoons, bread is eaten as sandwiches. And maybe more bread for an evening snack. One of the primary crops cultivated by the Taino was yuca or cassava, which they ate as a flatbread. This recipe has been documented as one that dates to precolonial times; it could be one of Borinquen's oldest. During that era, the yuca would be harvested, washed, peeled, and grated. Once the yuca was grated, the poisonous water would be squeezed from its "meat" and then that meat would be left out to dry until it had a flour-like consistency. Sometimes sea salt would be added to the flour, and the flour would be placed directly on a burén until it hardened, creating the bread. No water was added to the flour. I was fortunate to see this entire process at El Burén de Lula in Loíza.

This bread was—and still is—used for dipping into soups and stews long before rice ever touched the shores of Borinquen. Is it any wonder why Puerto Ricans love their pan?

2 large yuca

2 tablespoons salted butter, or as needed

Wash the tough, brown yuca skin and, using a knife or vegetable peeler, remove the exterior.

Place a box grater in a large bowl. Using the side with the smallest holes (the ones that protrude outward and are spiky), grate the yuca. Place about ¼ cup of the yuca in a large piece of cheesecloth or kitchen towel, forming a log shape. Roll up the log, with the yuca inside of the cheesecloth, then take either side of the cloth and twist the ends until they meet the yuca, squeezing out the water. Open the cheesecloth and break up the chunks of yuca with your fingers until it's loose and has a flour-like texture. Repeat with the remaining yuca.

Add a few teaspoons of the butter to a skillet and then add about ½ cup of the yuca "flour." Using the bottom of a measuring cup, press down on the mixture to compress it into a roundish, flat shape. Turn the heat to low and cook for 3 to 4 minutes, add another 1 teaspoon butter, flip, and cook the other side for 3 to 4 minutes, or until the casabe is golden brown. Transfer the casabe to a plate and repeat with the remaining yuca flour and butter.

Cut the casabe in half and serve immediately.

Note: I always use cast-iron skillets, which work well for casabe. Although I've seen this recipe made on a burén, I'm sure it would work in a nonstick pan as well.

Funche

Makes 4 to 6 servings

While my mom's 1976 Buick Regal warmed up in the long driveway of our casita, she would stand at our Wedgewood stove. It had a griddle in its center for pancakes, but on most days, my mom stood there stirring a corn mixture in her Corningware, keeping one eye on the pot and one eye on the rumbling car. I got dressed in front of the wall heater as the vapor pouring out of the car's tailpipe seemed to mingle with the steam from the stove until Mami spooned the mixture into a bowl, wrapped it with a kitchen towel, and set me and it in the backseat of the Regal. That's how I remember funche.

I'd eat spoonful after spoonful while staring out the still-foggy windows, the warm smell of cinnamon mixing with the used-book smell of the Regal's plush interior, a trail of brown sugar, evaporated milk, and specks of cinnamon waiting to be thoroughly combined with the softened cornmeal. My mother often made this on cold mornings for the journey to our eventual destination of school or Nina's house. For us, funche was affordable, hot, filling, and easy on the stomach. Turns out, this is exactly why Puerto Rican sugarcane plantation owners doled out funche to enslaved people generations ago. These days, I like to serve funche with Califas Shrimp (page 81). Mami does not approve.

2 cups water

1 cup ground polenta

1 (13.5-ounce) can coconut milk

Kosher salt

2 tablespoons salted butter

In a large saucepan over medium-high heat, bring 1½ cups of the water to a boil. Whisk in the polenta. When the mixture begins to thicken slightly, turn the heat to low and add half of the coconut milk. (You do not want the coconut milk to boil because it may separate.) Cover and cook for about 40 minutes, stirring every few minutes to prevent the polenta from sticking to the pan. Remove from the heat and whisk in the remaining coconut milk, then season with salt. If the polenta is still really thick, stir in the remaining ½ cup water.

Stir in the butter and serve immediately.

The Story of Funche

There are no grits in Puerto Rico. Not even as an import item. But cornmeal has been utilized by the inhabitants of the island since long before the conquistadors' baby blues sparkled on the horizon. Just as grits are mostly eaten for breakfast in the American South, funche is mostly eaten for breakfast by the older Puerto Ricans.

Crema de maiz is the United States' food industry's marketing name for funche; the only difference is the consistency. To make our lives easier, let's just say funche is Puerto Rican–style polenta: cornmeal cooked with water, milk, or coconut milk.

The relationship between Puerto Rico and corn goes back even further. Despite what many Statesiders assume is a love affair between Puerto Ricans and rice, corn was the staple that was essential to the indigenous Tainos who inhabited Borinquen long before Europeans landed. The Tainos planted and harvested corn in fertile soil and were even documented as preparing corn dumplings—forming and shaping dough, wrapping it in husks, and boiling or roasting it on an outdoor stove.

The Spanish watched the Tainos prepare corn in various ways and copied their techniques in creating a nutrient-dense porridge that would sustain them during their ambushes of other Caribbean islands. And in the nineteenth century, enslaved people on the sugar plantations were given funche. This is when the word, likely derived from the language of the African enslaved people, came into use. The porridge was paired with bacalao or melao de caña, a sugarcane syrup that was reduced until thick and dark brown.

Such eating habits continued through poorer populations of Puerto Rico into the twentieth century, when Puerto Ricans substituted funche for rice to be eaten with beans during extremely tough times. During the New Deal, processed cornmeal came in the monthly food subsidies of the Puerto Rico Emergency Relief Administration, along with things such as Spam and powdered eggs. Because of these food subsidies and the past consumption by enslaved people on the island, cornmeal became known as the food of the poor—the Black and Brown Puerto Ricans. Affluent Puerto Ricans (and those pretending to be) ceased consuming funche because of the stigma.

Of course, those who still eat funche prefer the processed boxed version as opposed to growing, drying, and grinding their own corn. Over the years, wheat flours have become the primary flour of choice on the island, while corn flour is more often used for sorullitos (fried corn fritters stuffed with cheese), guanimes (boiled corn dumplings), funche, and . . . nostalgia.

Salads and Sides

Have you caught on that Puerto Rican food is mostly brown on brown on brown and double-starch and meat? It is food meant to sustain a labor force, people. I understand how the cuisine can be thought of as heavy, and I also can see how my hatred of vegetables was formed. Yes, I dislike vegetables. There, I said it. I still eat them because I know they're good for me, but that doesn't mean I'm not cursing the day that Bibb lettuce was pulled from the ground with every bite I take. This chapter includes some of the vegetable sides that I've had to create to accompany my cooking for events.

The Pop-Up Salad

Makes 4 servings

When you're eating in a restaurant in Puerto Rico, a sad salad—limp lettuce and hard, barely red tomatoes—often accompanies your entrée, compliments of the Jones Act. When I'm cooking for pop-ups, I like to change that narrative. I know that Puerto Rican food can be rich and heavy. Double starch and meat. That can take a toll on most of the diners who attend my events. Fortunately, us Northern Californians have access to great avocados from Soledad, and heirloom tomatoes that are just waiting to be served as a chunky salad dressed with citrus and mint from our own backyards. (Sometimes I don't even chop the mint.)

2 large heirloom tomatoes,
cut into large chunks

2 avocados, cut into large chunks

Juice of 1 orange

Juice of 1 Meyer or regular lemon

10 leaves fresh mint,
coarsely chopped

1 tablespoon sofrito (see page 23)

Place the tomatoes and avocados in a large bowl. Set aside.

In another bowl, combine the orange juice, lemon juice, mint, and sofrito and mix well. Pour the juice mixture over the tomatoes and avocados.

Serve the salad immediately.

Tres Hermanas Sauté

Makes 2 to 4 servings

Tres hermanas, or the "three sisters" (also known as Hello, Summer!), are a centuries-old threesome—squash, corn, and climbing beans—that comprise the main agricultural yields of various Indigenous groups in the Americas. Originating in Mesoamerica, these crops were carried northward up the river valleys and used for food and trade. In a technique known as companion planting, they benefit from their proximity to one another. The corn gives the beans something to climb on. The beans provide nitrogen to the soil that the other plants use. The squash vines and leaves spread along the ground, blocking sunlight and helping prevent weeds that compete with the beans and corn for nutrients. The squash leaves also act as a living mulch, creating a microclimate that retains moisture in the soil while the vines' prickly hairs deter pests. Corn, beans, and squash contain complex carbohydrates, fatty acids, and all nine essential amino acids.

1 pound fresh green beans, coarsely diced

4 large ears corn, kernels removed from cobs

1 pound summer squash (zucchini, pattypan, or other varieties), coarsely diced

3 tablespoons salted butter

1 tablespoon Illyanna's Adobo (page 20)

Kosher salt

Freshly ground black pepper

Grated Parmesan cheese for garnishing

Fill a large bowl with water and ice. Set aside.

Bring a stockpot of salted water to a boil over high heat. Add the green beans and let boil for 1 to 3 minutes, or until they reach your desired tenderness. Using a fine-mesh strainer, scoop out the beans and transfer to the ice water. Add the corn and squash to the pot and let boil for 1 to 3 minutes, or until the squash has reached your desired tenderness. Scoop out the corn and squash and transfer to the ice water. Drain the water from the pot.

Place the pot back on the stove top, turn the heat to medium-high, add the butter and adobo, and season with salt and pepper. When the butter has melted, add the green beans, corn, and squash and stir to mix, ensuring the butter and seasoning have coated all the vegetables.

Serve the sauté in a large bowl and garnish with Parmesan cheese.

Note: This could easily be made with frozen or canned vegetables instead of fresh.

Cows in the fog, Rancho Llano Seco, Butte County, California.

Rancho Llano Seco.

Among the peach trees with Camelia Enriquez Miller, Twin Peaks Orchard, Placer County, California.

Cauliflower "Arroz" con Gandules

Makes 4 servings

My doctor once told me to lay off the rice. (I'm paraphrasing.) Personally, I want to eat white rice three times a day, every day. In the morning, I like it with eggs, watching the runny yolks coat the grains and appreciating the papery crackle of the fried edges. Lunch might easily be rice with a dash of soy sauce and salmon. Dinner could be rice with a rotisserie chicken that I grabbed from the grocery store because I was too tired to cook after returning home from the gym. I'll never tire of rice. This recipe is for all the rice lovers who want an alternate. Adding seasonings and gandules gives the cauliflower a more interesting texture and flavor. It's my basic attempt at trying to make cauliflower taste like something other than a Dutch oven—not the kind you cook with.

2 tablespoons olive oil

1 medium yellow onion, coarsely diced

1 (10-ounce) package frozen cauliflower rice

1 (15-ounce) can gandules

½ cup tomato sauce

¼ cup sofrito (see page 23)

2 tablespoons Illyanna's Adobo (page 20)

Add the olive oil to a wide skillet and place over medium-high heat. Add the onion and sauté for 3 to 4 minutes, or until softened. Add the cauliflower rice and continue to sauté for 2 to 3 minutes, then add the gandules, tomato sauce, sofrito, and adobo and stir to combine well. Let cook for 5 minutes.

Serve the cauliflower "arroz" from the skillet.

Guineos en Escabeche

Makes 6 to 8 servings

The first time that I served this dish (which was also the first time that I made it) was at my pop-up dinner at the now-defunct Doctor's Lounge in San Francisco's Outer Mission neighborhood. And just as I suspected, even those few who had eaten Puerto Rican food had never tried this before. I'd describe it as slightly resistant chunks of green bananas in a spiky vinegar and oniony sauce. It's one of those offerings that's an acquired taste, and the only time that I have ever seen it out in the wild is at a few lechoneras in the Guavate neighborhood in Cayey, Puerto Rico.

Remember to use a pot that you don't particularly care about the appearance of, because the guineos will stain it as they boil.

2 pounds guineos

1 cup olive oil

½ cup distilled white vinegar

8 garlic cloves

1 tablespoon freshly ground black pepper

1 teaspoon ground cumin

3 dried bay leaves

3 shallots, thinly sliced

Kosher salt

Bring a large pot of water to a boil over high heat. Add the guineos and let boil for 13 to 20 minutes, or until the skins have separated from the flesh and the water turns black. Using tongs, remove the guineos from the pot and set aside to cool. Once they're cool, remove the peels, cut into 1-inch-thick medallions, and place on a serving plate.

Add the olive oil to a small pot and place over medium-low heat. Add the vinegar, garlic, black pepper, cumin, and bay leaves and poach to infuse the oil. Do not let the oil boil; you may have to adjust the heat level to keep the oil warm. Turn off the heat, add the shallots to the infused oil, and season with salt.

Pour the infused oil over the guineo medallions. Let sit to absorb the oil for at least 20 minutes or up to overnight in the fridge.

Serve the guineos cold or at room temperature.

Maduros

Makes 4 to 6 servings

I don't think my nana liked tostones or maduros much; I don't ever remember seeing her make them. Which means that Mami never cooked either of them at home. I have eaten fried sweet plantains in plenty of Caribbean and South American cooking, but all of them were lackluster—tough and not even close to being sweet enough. When I started cooking, I found out that they were underwhelming through no fault of their own, as it's difficult to consistently find enough perfectly ripe amarillos needed for restaurant service. And frozen maduros are not readily available on the West Coast.

The first time that I ate memorable maduros was at a now-defunct Puerto Rican food truck in Oakland (the Bay Area's first Puerto Rican food truck). Whether they used frozen or fresh amarillos, there was no denying the intoxicating, sweet incense. They were blackened, sticky, and caramelized around the edges and custardy in the middle, offsetting the cumbersome heaviness of double starch and meat. Just as my taste buds got tired, here came the maduros to sweep me off my feet. I still haven't had maduros as good as the ones from that food truck.

3 super-ripe amarillos (see "Peeling Guineos and Plátanos," page 12)

Canola oil for frying

Kosher salt

Peel the amarillos and cut on the diagonal into ¾-inch-thick slices.

Line a plate with paper towels and set near the stove. Fill a 10-inch cast-iron skillet with 1 inch of canola oil and place over medium-high heat. You want enough oil to slightly cover the amarillos. Heat the oil until it reaches 350°F on an instant-read thermometer. (Add a tiny piece of amarillo; if the oil sizzles, it's ready for frying.)

Add the amarillos to the oil and fry on one side for 2 to 5 minutes, or until the edges start to brown. Using tongs or a slotted spoon, flip them and fry for 2 to 3 minutes more. Transfer the slices to the prepared plate and sprinkle with salt while hot.

Serve the maduros immediately.

Viandas

Makes 4 servings

Simply put, these are boiled root vegetables. Viandas are often eaten with rich meats, fried foods, or, more commonly, bacalao. To my memory, the only time that I ever saw my mother and grandmother cooking together is when they made bacalao ensalada (see page 87) and viandas. And I never saw anyone else eat viandas except Mami and Nana. I think Mami felt the most nourishment from Nana when they'd make this meal. They made the bacalao ensalada just the way my mom liked it: shredded bacalao and thinly sliced raw white onions, then garnished with black pepper and a good dousing of olive oil, with a side of root vegetables that had been boiled in salted water. Some would call it plain, but I think it's simple perfection.

3 Yukon gold potatoes

1 large garnet yam

1 large purple yautía (also known as yautía lila or malanga lila)

1 large yuca

1 large plátano, peeled (see page 12)

Kosher salt

Bring a large pot of salted water to a rolling boil over high heat.

Peel the potatoes, yam, yautía, and yuca and cut them into quarters. Add the yuca to the water and let boil for 15 minutes. Then add the potatoes, yam, and yautía and let boil for 10 to 15 minutes more, or until all are fork-tender (be sure to test the yuca and potato). Add the plátano and let boil for 5 to 10 minutes, or until fork-tender. Gently transfer the contents of the pot into a colander, discarding the water. Remove and discard the woody stem from the center of the yuca.

Transfer the viandas to a serving dish, season with salt, and serve.

Mofongo

Makes 2 servings

Technically, this is a *bi*fongo. I use the ripeness of the amarillo to give moisture to the mofongo instead of constantly adding seasoned water as some other cooks do. You could use any number of toppings for mofongo. Some people use fried chicken, carne frita (fried pork chunks), carne guisada, or pollo guisado. The sauces have gotten completely wild with people using mayoketchup (see page 20), garlic cream sauces, or mornay sauce. And sometimes the mofongo is just served on its own in a bowl of chicken broth. You want to make these in small batches to save wear and tear on your hands and arms.

Canola oil for frying

2 plátanos, peeled (see "Peeling Guineos and Plátanos," page 12) and sliced into 1-inch-thick medallions

1 amarillo, peeled (see page 12) and sliced into 1-inch-thick medallions

5 garlic cloves, minced

¼ cup chicharrones (optional)

2 teaspoons garlic powder

Kosher salt

1 tablespoon water

1 tablespoon sofrito (see page 23)

Chicharron de Pollo (page 103) for topping

Line a plate with paper towels and set near the stove. Fill a 10-inch cast-iron skillet with ½ inch of canola oil and place over medium-high heat. You want enough oil to submerge the plátanos and amarillo. Heat the oil until it registers 350°F on an instant-read thermometer. (Add a tiny piece of plátano; if the oil sizzles, it's ready for frying.)

Add the plátanos and amarillo in the oil and fry for 5 to 7 minutes, or until soft. Using tongs or a slotted spoon, transfer the medallions to the prepared plate. Set aside.

In a pilón, molcajete, or a large bowl, mash one of the garlic cloves, pounding until it has disintegrated and is sticky. Add the remaining garlic, fried plátano and amarillo, chicharrones (if using), and garlic powder; season with salt; and mash. Then add the water, mash again, add the sofrito, and mash one final time. (Do this in stages if your pilón isn't large enough for one go.)

Pack about ½ cup mofongo into a teacup or small bowl. Invert onto a serving plate to unmold. Repeat to make the remaining servings. Top the mounds with pollo and serve immediately.

Mofongo Dressing with Salami

Makes 2 to 4 servings

Mofongo dressing is not something that ever made an appearance on my nana's or my mother's Thanksgiving tables. I merged the already existing mofongo dressing with bits of my mother's cornbread dressing (see page 190) to create this recipe for Friendsgiving one year. The dish is one way to introduce friends to Puerto Rican culture. And since not everyone is on board with the dressing being cooked inside the bird, Mofongo Dressing with Salami is a sure way to please everyone, combining the nostalgia of family memories and the sabor of birthright.

Canola oil for frying

6 plátanos, peeled (see page 12) and sliced into 1-inch-thick medallions

¼ cup olive oil

1 cup diced hard salami

½ cup sofrito (see page 23)

Kosher salt

Freshly ground black pepper

1 cup water or low-sodium chicken broth, or as needed

Preheat the oven to 375°F.

Line a baking sheet with paper towels and set near the stove. Fill a 10-inch cast-iron skillet with ½ inch of canola oil and place over medium-high heat. You want enough oil to partially submerge the plátanos. Heat the oil until it registers 350°F on an instant-read thermometer. (Add a tiny piece of plátano; if the oil sizzles, it's ready for frying.)

Add the plátanos, in batches, to the oil and fry for 5 to 7 minutes, or until tender, using tongs to flip them. Transfer the medallions to the prepared baking sheet.

Add the olive oil to another large cast-iron skillet and place over medium-high heat. Add the salami and fry for 4 to 6 minutes, or until crispy, golden, and softened. Remove the pan from the heat and set aside, keeping the salami and the oil in the pan.

In a large bowl, combine the fried plátanos and sofrito, season with salt and pepper, and mash with a potato masher until combined but still chunky, adding the water, 1 to 2 tablespoons at a time, just as needed to soften the mixture—it should not be liquidy. (The amount of water needed will vary depending on how ripe the plátanos are—firmer, greener ones will need more water.) Fold in the salami and oil from the skillet until thoroughly combined. Add more water, if needed, until the mixture is moist but still somewhat stiff. Transfer the mixture to the cast-iron skillet and bake, uncovered, for 12 to 15 minutes, or until the top just starts to brown.

Serve the dressing from the skillet.

Maisonet's Cornbread and Salami Dressing

Makes 8 servings

My family's Northern California Thanksgiving table was always covered with the traditional fixings: a gargantuan supermarket turkey, ploppy jellied cranberry sauce, mashed potatoes, buttered rolls, and sweet potatoes that came in a purple can. Those sweet potatoes were subsequently topped with marshmallows and roasted, and they found their way farther and farther to the back of the buffet, untouched. In retrospect, I feel sad for those sweet potatoes.

At Thanksgiving, my mother always makes Nana's cornbread dressing—a combination of Jiffy Corn Muffin mix and hefty chunks of San Francisco Bay Area–born Gallo salami. Both my mother and my grandmother exclusively used the salami that comes in a log, which Gallo calls "the chub"—it's a dry Italian salami in a cylindrical shape, wrapped in paper, and sealed at both ends with metal crimps. Using the salami chub is an anomaly that my nana picked up from her Italian neighbor back in the 1950s. To my grandmother, newly arrived from Puerto Rico, a sausage was a sausage was a sausage. (Vintage Puerto Ricans love to add pork flavoring to just about everything.) In a flash, she had changed the landscape of the recipes of her motherland out of necessity, making it Californian–Puerto Rican.

The Cali-Rican approach lives on in my kitchen. Standing over the stove, I take in the huge waft of salami perfume when it hits the hot oil in the pan and the fat combines with the onion, celery, and garlic. Although it's me who's doing the cooking, when I'm looking into the pan, I feel like I'm my mom or grandma at the stove—a feeling that I hope will stay with me when Mami's long gone.

2 (8.5-ounce) boxes Jiffy Corn Muffin Mix

½ cup unsalted butter

1 (8- to 10-ounce) salami, cut into ½-inch pieces

1 large yellow onion, cut into ½-inch pieces

3 celery stalks, cut into ½-inch pieces

5 garlic cloves, chopped

Kosher salt

Freshly ground black pepper

3 tablespoons finely chopped sage

1 (5- to 7-ounce) bag stuffing-mix croutons

4 cups low-sodium chicken broth

A night or two before you plan to serve the dressing, prepare the muffin mix, following the instructions on the box to make cornbread. Let the cornbread cool completely, then break into 1-inch chunks and place on a baking sheet at room temperature, uncovered, to air-dry.

When ready to prepare the dressing, preheat the oven to 350°F and butter a 9 by 1-inch baking dish.

Add 1 tablespoon of the butter to a large skillet and place over medium heat. Add the salami and cook, tossing often, for about 4 minutes, or until lightly browned. Using a slotted spoon, transfer the salami to a large bowl.

Add 4 tablespoons butter to the skillet. When the butter has melted, add the onion, celery, and garlic and season with salt and pepper. Cook, stirring occasionally, for 10 to 12 minutes, or until very soft. Add the sage and toss to combine.

Add the croutons and cornbread to the salami and gently toss to combine. Then add the vegetable mixture and any butter remaining in the skillet and gently toss again. Drizzle the chicken broth over everything and let it soak into the cornbread. Season with salt and pepper and gently toss until just combined (overmixing will cause the cornbread to fall apart); season with more salt and pepper if needed. The dressing should be moist, but there shouldn't be any liquid pooling in the bottom of bowl.

Transfer the dressing to the prepared baking dish. Melt the remaining 3 tablespoons butter and drizzle over the top. Bake 40 to 45 minutes, or until golden brown on top and bottom.

Serve the dressing immediately.

Sweets and Drinks

I wouldn't say desserts are a huge thing in Puerto Rico. Being able to consume certain desserts was exclusive to the affluent class. The Spanish introduced many a pastry created with butter or manteca from their native land and combined local tropical fruits from their new homeland, leaving a gastronomic impression that can be found in the storefront windows of various bakeries throughout the island. Quesitos and pastelillos. Brazo gitanos and panetelas. Flan and tembleque. Dulce de coco and mampostial. And the influence of the States has left an even bigger and more addictive legacy of manufactured sweets, mass-produced candy, processed snack cakes, and even doughnuts. No matter if it's Donas Aymat—the local version of Hostess—or the homemade sugar-coated version from regional vendors who bake in obscurity, doughnuts have found their way into the hearts of Puerto Ricans.

I don't remember my grandma baking much. I don't even know if she had the opportunity to bake before coming to the States. My mom has some memories of Nana baking birthday cakes without measurements, before boxed mixes hit the scene, and making simple confectioners' sugar–water icings and glazes. Where my grandma picked up these ideas, who's to know? I never thought to ask her about baking; she did it so seldomly. She came from the campo, where things are cooked outside on a fogon, which is basically a woodfire setup. Chuckwagon-style. People who go car-camping have fun setting up and cooking outside while they're roughing it for a few days, but cooking over a wood fire was Grandma's everyday life.

Opposite, inset: Don Chire selling donas, Cabo Rojo, Puerto Rico.

Persimmon Cookies

Makes 30 cookies

Persimmon cookies are one of two dessert recipes that I remember my grandma baking. The other was an upside-down pineapple cake, which she prepared from a boxed mix. She made both without a recipe or precise measurements. For my family, these cookies would not be authentic if the Hachiya persimmons came from anywhere else but Katie's yard. Katie came from Croatia in the 1950s to live with her husband a few blocks from Nana's townhouse. We have been buying persimmons from Katie since before I started elementary school. It was in front of Katie's house, on the way back from Kmart, that Nana stopped the cart she "borrowed" from the store and told me, "Aye, Mija. You're too heavy to push." It was a pivotal moment in growing up in an otherwise extended adolescence during which Mami and Nana babied me longer than is customary.

Katie is now in her nineties, frail, and legally blind. During the autumn, I help her pick the surreal plump persimmons from her century-old tree. Katie can't see the persimmons from far away, so she clumsily searches the branches and leaves until her hands happen upon one of the burnt-orange globes. We talk a while after picking, and she always asks, "What are you going to make with them?" And I always reply, "Cookies." I'll make the same dense and chewy cookies that Nana made. The dough will be laced with an abundance of spices and my own addition of cardamom, straying from Nana's version. But she's not here to scold me, and Katie says she won't be here much longer either.

1 to 3 super-ripe Hachiya persimmons

½ cup salted butter,
at room temperature

½ cup granulated sugar

1 egg

1 cup all-purpose flour

2 teaspoons pumpkin pie spice

½ teaspoon baking soda

¼ teaspoon ground cardamom

¼ teaspoon kosher salt

½ cup chopped walnuts

Preheat the oven to 350°F. Line a baking sheet with parchment paper.

Remove and discard the tops of the persimmons. Slice open the persimmons and scoop out the insides with a soupspoon, saving the pulp in a bowl. Discard any seeds. Finely chop the persimmon skin and add to the pulp. Spoon the persimmon pulp, skin, and juice into a glass measuring cup; you need 1 cup total.

In a large bowl, using a rubber spatula, vigorously cream the butter for 30 seconds. (You can also use a stand mixer with the paddle attachment at medium speed.) Add the sugar, and cream with the butter for 30 seconds, or until pale yellow and airy. Add the egg and persimmon and beat about 1 minute more, or until fully combined.

In a medium bowl, combine the flour, pumpkin pie spice, baking soda, cardamom, and salt. Add the walnuts and stir to mix. Fold the flour mixture into the persimmon mixture, mixing everything until the flour disappears and you have a thick batter.

Using a tablespoon, spoon the dough in equal-size mounds onto the prepared baking sheet, about ½ inch apart. Bake for 10 to 15 minutes, or until the cookies are puffy and dark brown. Place the baking sheet on a wire rack to cool.

Store the cookies in an airtight container for up to 2 days.

Coconut Soda–Pineapple Upside-Down Cake

Makes 8 to 12 servings

When Nana made pineapple upside-down cake, she would coat the baking pan with margarine and brown sugar and line it with canned pineapple rings and maraschino cherries. She also added 7UP to the boxed cake mix. She poured the batter over the pineapple and cherries and baked it until the cake was golden brown and firm in the center. Unforgettable. Much to the chagrin of Chef Teresa Urkofsky, my mentor and former pastry instructor, I love boxed mixes. I make an upside-down pineapple cake with guava and cream cheese frosting for all my pop-ups and private dinners. I have always been so surprised by the number of people who say they don't like cake. But those diners liked *my* cake. Whether they were just being polite or I had truly converted them, the world will never know. The confession is . . . those cakes for private dinners were always made with a boxed cake mix.

3 tablespoons salted butter

½ cup packed dark brown sugar

1 (15.25-ounce) box yellow cake mix (preferably Pillsbury Moist Supreme)

1 (3.4-ounce) box coconut cream pudding mix (preferably Jell-O Instant)

1 cup coconut soda or lemon-lime soda (preferably Coco Rico or 7UP)

¾ cup vegetable oil

3 eggs

1 medium pineapple, peeled, halved, cored, and sliced lengthwise into 2-inch-wide planks

Preheat the oven to 350°F. Line an 8-inch square baking pan with aluminum foil.

Put the butter and brown sugar in the prepared pan, spread into an even layer, and put in the oven for 15 minutes, or until the sugar starts to bubble.

In a large bowl, combine the cake mix, pudding mix, soda, vegetable oil, and eggs and stir to mix. Set aside.

Remove the baking pan from the oven and swirl it around to ensure the butter and sugar are incorporated. Lay the pineapple planks in the pan, arranging them snugly together to fully cover the bottom. Pour the cake batter over the pineapple slices and smooth the top with a butter knife.

Bake for 25 to 30 minutes, or until the cake is dark golden brown (I take my bakes a little darker than most) and a toothpick inserted in the center comes out clean. Top the pan with a wire cooling rack and invert the cake over a baking sheet (to catch any errant caramel). Let cool for 5 minutes and then remove the foil.

Cut the cake into pieces and serve from the pan.

Note: You can store leftover cake, loosely covered, at room temperature for up to 3 days.

A coconut ice-cream cone, King's Cream, Ponce, Puerto Rico.

Maria Lao, King's Cream.

A King's Cream regular.

King's Cream flavors.

TAMARINDO

LIMÓN

MANÍ

MANGO

Los Chinos de Ponce

Los Chinos de Ponce ice-cream shops are an enduring part of the food culture across the island. Most of the shops are modest—a single room—with takeout being the only option. Some of them have been remodeled while others have preserved their midcentury-modern pastel decor. The typical commercial ice-cream dipping cabinet is front and center. King's Cream and Rex Cream are the more famous of the parlors, with various outlets scattered around Puerto Rico, all owned by someone in one of the island's Chinese Cuban families.

Angel Pons, who is Chinese Cuban, started King's Cream in 1962. Two years later, Pons sold the business to Mario Lao. Mardie Lao, who is married to Mario Lao's son, Mario Junior, explains that Angel Pons was "just a Chinese businessman" who may have worked at Trader Vic's, where Don Mario met him. Together, the Laos have been running King's Cream since 1983.

Other shops have similar stories. In the early 1960s, Alfredo Louk, another Chinese Cuban immigrant, also opened an ice-cream shop. Louk was a native of Canton (Guangzhou) who lost everything to the Communist regime in Cuba, so he moved to Puerto Rico and married Violeta Louk (née Chang) in 1963. Violeta was Chinese but born and raised in Cuba's high society. According to her daughter, Aileen Louk, the family opened the first Rex Cream in 1963. Second, third, and fourth stores soon followed. More than a half century later, the Louks are still running Rex Cream, with Aileen at the helm for the last twenty-four years.

These natural-fruit ice-cream shops became a huge sensation and destination for Puerto Ricans, who called them los helados de Chinos because they were known to be owned by Chinese immigrants. You can still see Chinese characters on some of the shops' older signs.

Depending on what local fruits are available, most of the ice-cream flavors skew toward the tropical options that Puerto Ricans recognize: tamarind, mango, coconut, banana, parcha (passion fruit), guanabana (soursop), pineapple, and some classic hits such as vanilla, chocolate, strawberry, almond, and peanut butter. But one of the most popular flavors is corn ice cream topped with a generous sprinkling of cinnamon. The result tastes like a frozen form of funche (see page 174), Puerto Rico's answer to warm farina to which cinnamon and brown sugar are usually added.

continued ▶

The ice cream at both Rex and King's Cream doesn't feature the typical ice-cream texture. They're made in the method of gelato, so the consistency is such. You can watch the employees of both businesses make the ice cream throughout the day right at the counter. When the employees place an oar-size paddle into the ice-cream mixture as it spins in a deep metal-tube container, centrifugal force pushes the ice cream up the paddle. The ice cream is then placed into another metal container for service. Most of the modern ice-cream machinery comes from Italy and is made by a company called Cattabriga.

The ice cream is soft; the flavors are pure. There is no middleman with these stores. The shops buy the raw ingredients—sugar, fruit, peanut butter— and then make the ice cream. If they can't access these products, they don't make that flavor. Between the cooks and the ingredients, these are recipes that could come to fruition only here.

Aileen and Violeta Louk, Rex Cream, Guayama, Puerto Rico.

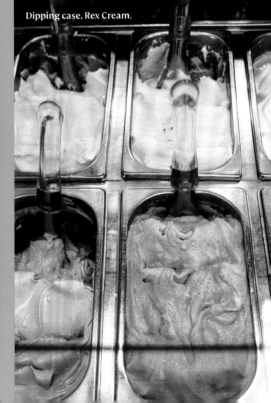

Rex Cream flavors.

Sabores

Vainilla	Vanilla
coco	coconut
fresa	strawberry
chocolate	chocolate
bizcocho	cake
chocolate chip	chocolate chip
almendra	almond
Pistachio	Pistachio
maíz	corn
oreo Galleta	cookies n cream
mani	Peanut butter
limón	lime
Guayaba	Guava
Parcha	Passion fruit
Guanabana	soursop
Piña	Pineapple
acerola	barbados cherry
tamarindo	tamarind

VASOS ⊚ BARQUILLAS ⊚ Batidas

Gracias por su visita

REX CREAM

Aileen Louk, Rex Cream, Guayama, Puerto Rico.

Dipping case, Rex Cream.

The Story of Brazo Gitano

When the Andalusians arrived in Puerto Rico, they were some of the richest people in the world. And in Puerto Rico, they had free labor at their beck and call. But they didn't have the gastronomic comforts of their home. It wasn't long before they improvised with local resources. Brazo gitanos (which translates to "gypsy's arm") could not be made with the fruits they were used to back in Spain. So, they used the fruits available on the island. This is how we got guava-filled brazo gitano, the island's most popular rolled-cake flavor.

Brazo gitano is a cake that can contain as few as four ingredients: flour, eggs, sugar, and vanilla. There is no rising agent (whipping egg whites to soft peaks and folding them into beaten yolks gives the cake its height and airiness). But there are some who take shortcuts, opting to skip the egg separation and whipping method.

The cake is said to have gotten its name in early-nineteenth-century Spain, when traveling boilermakers passed through the patisseries of the cities, according to Joan Turull I Estatuet, president of the Pastisseria Guild of Barcelona and owner of Pastisseria Turull near Barcelona. The boilermakers created utensils and kitchenware for bakeries; they would receive leftover cuts of cake along with their pay. "Because their hands were filthy, they'd rest the cake on their forearms. The bakers noticed the odd placement of the cake, and the cake was forever known as brazo gitano," Estauet explained.

Another theory for the cake's origin stems from the pionono cake in Granada, a city in southern Spain's Andalusia region. In 1897, pionono—a filled and rolled cake—became all the rage when a bakery created it to pay homage to Pope Pius IX, according to local baker Pastelerías Casa Isla's website. (In Puerto Rico, a pionono is a savory dish with picadillo encased by amarillos, dipped in egg, and fried.) Casa Isla turns each slice filled-side down, bathes it in a simple syrup, and tops it with a sweet custard that's brûléed, giving it the look of a pope's hat.

Whatever the inspiration, one of the most popular brazo gitano bakeries, Franco Brazo Gitano, in Puerto Rico dates to 1900; E. Franco & Co. opened it in Mayagüez (known as the "place of waters" to the Taino). The business still stands in its original brick building, which survived the 1918 San Fermín earthquake. It is salmon pink—the hue subdued by time—surrounded by brightly colored buildings that are decorated with ornamental wrought iron and black-and-white-checkered tile floors.

Brazo Gitano with Burge Road Cherry Cream Filling

Makes 6 to 12 servings

I have some of the most beautiful produce in the world readily accessible in my backyard, but when I got a hankering to make my own brazo gitano, I didn't have easy access to local guava. Remembering that the Brazo Gitano Franco bakery in Mayagüez has a cherry-filled cake, I figured the next best thing to guava was local cherries. That's how I stumbled on a cherry orchard in Stockton, California. Little did I know what a great story it had.

Jontue and Oscar Grado are the two young farmers who own Burge Road Farm. They are the epitome of Stockton's agricultural history. Jontue descends from Filipino ancestors; Oscar, who is Mexican and Puerto Rican, is a U.S. Army veteran. Filipinos and Mexicans were the main farm labor force in Stockton from as early as the 1930s through the 1960s, and eventually joined forces in the 1960s during the Delano Grape Strike, fighting together for farmworkers' rights. This was the social justice action that brought the most attention to the United Farm Workers movement, led by Cesar Chavez and Larry Itliong.

The Grados bought the cherry and walnut orchard in 2014, mostly so their family could live a quieter way of life. It might have been a quieter lifestyle, but it definitely wasn't an easier one. "He grew up having fond memories of climbing and picking fruit trees at his grandpa Tom's house and tagging along with his family when they did seasonal jobs picking produce in the fields of Stockton," Jontue told me about Oscar. And because Oscar already had some experience with trees—his father has owned a tree service company in Stockton for thirty years—running the farm seemed like a no-brainer.

The two took notice that family and friends loved coming into the orchard and picking fruit from the trees. In 2015, the Grados decided to open their farm to the public for U-pick during the early-summer peak cherry season. They were surprised by the overwhelming response of patrons who wanted to pick their own. The U-pick concept seemed perfect, especially since they considered themselves too small to compete with the surrounding cherry producers. And they loved the idea of sharing their farm with families who wanted to get closer to the earth, be in the sunshine, and have fun picking directly from the trees.

On the day that Mami and I visited Burge Road Farm, we drove down a narrow strip of asphalt that cut a makeshift road through old walnut, almond, and cherry trees. The friction between the tires of the car and the ancient earth created trails of airborne dust and left a storm behind us. Once in the orchard, we zigzagged from tree to tree, searching through the bright green leaves for the cherries; some were fire-engine red and others the color of Cabernet Sauvignon. Although it had rained furiously just two weeks before, giving some of the fruit fatal cracks at their seams, it was one of those typical sweltering summer days in the Central Valley. Our hard work as U-pickers paid off. Those were some of the best cherries that we'd had in a very long time. After a while, we didn't notice the heat as we sat under trees at the far end of the orchard. I sat on the ground; my bare feet exposed. Shade was plentiful, and the breeze swept right over us as we ate our sun-warmed fruit. I found it magical; so much so that I had tricked myself into picking five pounds of cherries in no time. Being able to consume only so many fresh cherries, I decided that making jam would be a good way to preserve their beautiful flavor—a jam that would be perfect for my own brazo gitano filling later in the year when there would be no fresh cherries. Puerto Rico meets Northern California.

1 cup coarsely chopped pitted ripe cherries (see Note)

1 lemon wedge

5 eggs, separated

1/3 cup granulated sugar, plus 1/4 cup

1 pinch kosher salt

2 tablespoons unsalted butter, melted

1 1/2 tablespoons milk

10 tablespoons cake flour, sifted

1 teaspoon baking powder

2 cups cream cheese, at room temperature

2 cups confectioners' sugar, plus more for dusting

Preheat the oven to 325°F. Lightly butter and flour a 10 1/2 by 15 1/2-inch jelly-roll pan.

Put the cherries in a bowl and squish them with your hands. Squeeze the juice from the lemon wedge over the cherries and set aside to macerate.

In a large bowl, using an electric mixer (or with a whisk), whip the egg whites on high speed for 30 seconds, or until foamy. Gradually add the 1/3 cup granulated sugar and continue to whip for 5 to 7 minutes, or until stiff peaks form. Set aside. Clean the mixer beaters (or whisk).

Put the egg yolks in a separate bowl. Add the salt and remaining 1/4 cup granulated sugar and whip for 3 to 4 minutes, or until the yolks are pale yellow and fall in ribbons from the beaters (or whisk). Add the melted butter and milk to the yolk mixture and beat on high speed for 1 to 2 minutes. Add the flour and baking powder and mix for 1 to 2 minutes, or until thoroughly incorporated into a batter.

With a rubber spatula, fold one-third of the egg whites into the batter, until no streaks of egg white are seen. Repeat with the remaining egg whites, folding them in one-third at a time. Pour the cake batter into the prepared pan.

continued ▶

Bake for 15 minutes, or until a toothpick inserted in the center comes out clean. Place the pan on a wire rack to cool for 10 to 15 minutes. Then cover the entire cake with a clean kitchen towel and invert the pan to release the cake onto the towel. Use the towel to roll up the cake and then set the cake in the towel on the wire rack for about 30 minutes, or until cooled completely. This step will give the cake muscle memory for holding its shape after it's filled. Leave it rolled up until it's completely cool and you've finished making the filling.

In a large bowl, using a wooden spoon, combine the cream cheese, confectioners' sugar, cherries, and most of the juice they've produced. The mixture should have spreadable consistency; if it doesn't, incorporate more cherry juice, 1 tablespoon at a time, until it does.

Unroll the cake, leaving it on the towel. Spread as much of the cream cheese mixture as you can over the cake, leaving a 1-inch border along the ends and the long side farthest from you. Starting with the long side closest to you, roll up the cake. Dust with confectioners' sugar. Using the towel as a sling, transfer the cake to a serving platter, positioning it seam-side down.

Using a serrated knife, cut the brazo gitano into slices and serve. It is best eaten the day it is made.

Note: There's no easy way to pit cherries. Either you have one of those little gadgets that pits them for you, or you just smash the shit out of them on a cutting board in the same way you'd smash garlic. And if you can't access fresh cherries, use the same amount of great-quality cherry preserves!

Strawberry Shortcakes

Makes 12 servings

You're thinking, "Yo! This is not a Puerto Rican recipe, and it sure as hell ain't a shortcake." But Nana would make these every spring when strawberries would flood the supermarket, stacked and nestled, mostly red and flavorless, under the fluorescent lighting bouncing off the grocer's glossy floors. Because of corporate ingenuity, Nana paired those mostly substandard strawberries with the small, yellow sponge cakes that were upsold as "shortcakes perfect for strawberries!" Add a dollop of Cool Whip (because ain't no one got enough money for the shit in the can, and how would a Puerto Rican born in 1938 know the damn difference?), and you've got yourself a relatively affordable quick-fix disguised as something healthful because, you know . . . strawberries.

Don't just assume that strawberry season is limited to spring. True, some varieties are available as soon as late March, but some of the sweetest strawberries are ready when the last rain starts to fall and cossets the delicate fronds of the wild fennel that monopolizes the sides of backroads and riverbanks, releasing their black licorice perfume into openness. So many strawberry-field stands and U-picks are owned by Hmong immigrants in Sacramento's surrounding area, making it effortless for locals to access strawberries at their peak ripeness and juiciest just a few miles down the road.

Sweetened Berries

1 pound fresh or frozen strawberries

¼ cup granulated sugar (see Note)

Shortcakes

8 tablespoons margarine, at room temperature

1 cup granulated sugar

½ cup almond milk

2 eggs

1 teaspoon vanilla extract

1½ cups all-purpose flour

2 teaspoons baking powder

1 pinch kosher salt

Whipped Cream

1 cup heavy whipping cream

1 tablespoon granulated sugar (see Note)

½ teaspoon vanilla extract

To prepare the berries: Slice the strawberries in half and place in a bowl. Sprinkle in the sugar and, with your hands, roughly smash the berries. Set aside. (The strawberries can be stored in an airtight container in the fridge for up to 3 days.)

To make the shortcakes: Preheat the oven to 350°F. Generously butter the cups of a twelve-well muffin tin.

In a large bowl, combine the margarine and sugar and, using a rubber spatula, cream until thoroughly incorporated. Add the almond milk, eggs, and vanilla and stir to combine well. Add the flour, baking powder, and salt and fold the dry ingredients into the wet ingredients until just combined. Divide the batter among the prepared muffin cups.

Bake for 12 to 15 minutes, or until golden brown and a toothpick inserted in the center of one of the shortcakes comes out clean. Set the pan on a wire cooling rack. (The shortcakes can be stored in an airtight container at room temperature for up to 3 days.)

To make the whipped cream: In a large bowl, using an electric mixer or a large whisk, whip together the heavy whipping cream, sugar, and vanilla for 2 to 4 minutes, or until it turns thick and stiff peaks form. (The whipped cream can be stored in an airtight container in the fridge for up to 2 days.)

When ready to serve, run a knife around the edge of the shortcakes and pop them out of the tin. Place the cakes on individual serving plates. Press the centers of the cakes, creating indentations and top each with a spoonful of strawberries and a dollop of whipped cream.

Note: The amount of sugar necessary to sweeten the strawberries will differ depending on where you're getting them, how ripe they are, and how much sugar you like! Obviously, if they're super-ripe, you won't need ¼ cup sugar. You can also use a lot more strawberries if you prefer; it won't affect the outcome. You can also add more sugar to your whipping cream.

Ron del Barrilito Rum Cake

Makes 1 (10-inch) tube or Bundt cake

This is not traditional in any sense. It's a little all over the place with nods of acknowledgment to several cake specialties across the island. It's soaked in Puerto Rico's oldest rum. The spices and a splash of grape juice are in tribute to Añasco's specialty, bizcocho de hojaldre. For some reason, *hojaldre* translates to "puff pastry," even though it's not puff pastry at all—it's a cake batter. Of course, the original hojaldre recipe is extremely elusive, as it's been passed down from generation to generation in a storytelling format, the way Puerto Ricans love to relay information. For this recipe, I used the traditional tube cake pan, a Bundt-style pan without the ridges, but you can use any 10-inch, high-sided pan you have.

1½ cups all-purpose flour

1 cup granulated sugar

2 tablespoons pumpkin pie spice

1 tablespoon baking powder

¼ teaspoon kosher salt

¼ teaspoon cream of tartar

⅓ cup vegetable shortening, at room temperature

⅓ cup milk, plus 2 tablespoons

2 tablespoons concord grape juice

2 eggs

1 teaspoon vanilla extract

Rum Syrup

1½ cups granulated sugar

1½ cups margarine

¾ cup gold rum (preferably Ron del Barrilito 2 Star)

¼ cup water

2 cups walnuts, finely chopped

Preheat the oven to 350°F. Butter a 10-inch tube cake pan.

In a large bowl, using a spatula, combine the flour, sugar, pumpkin pie spice, baking powder, salt, cream of tartar, shortening, ⅓ cup milk, and grape juice. (Alternatively, mix in a stand mixer with the paddle attachment, beating for 2 to 3 minutes.) Beat in the eggs and vanilla, combining well for 1 to 2 minutes. Pour the batter into the prepared pan.

Bake for 40 to 50 minutes, or until the edges are dark, the cake has pulled away from the sides of the pan, and a toothpick inserted in the center comes out clean. Set on a wire rack to cool.

To make the syrup: In a small pan over medium heat, combine the sugar, margarine, rum, and water. Let simmer for about 25 minutes, or until the sugar and margarine have melted and the mixture has transformed into a syrup.

Leaving the cake in the baking pan, poke holes all over the cake while it is still warm. Gradually pour 1 cup of the warm syrup over the cake (this is the bottom). Once the liquid has been absorbed, place a serving platter over the cake pan and flip onto the platter. Poke holes into the top of the cake and pour the remaining syrup over it.

Sprinkle the walnuts over the top while the syrup is still warm, wet, and sticky. Let the cake set for 5 to 10 minutes and then cut into wedges to serve.

Note: You can store leftover cake, uncovered, at room temperature for up to 3 days.

Pastelillos de Yellow Peaches

Makes 9 pastelillos

Summer in most of Northern California is like summer in Hades. Temperatures often reach the triple digits. The cottonwood trees release their gossamer fairies just as the heavy winds and fire season start to pick up. The good news is that we know peaches and nectarines are on the horizon. In this recipe, I like to use ripe yellow peaches or yellow nectarines, which I can get directly from Twin Peaks Orchard, a farm that was founded by Yoshichika and Tomeo Nakae in 1912. The orchard is still family-owned and operated by Camelia Enriquez Miller, who does most of the day-to-day work. The day that Mami and I visited Camelia, we hopped onto her ATV and she hauled ass through the trees while pointing out multiple varieties of yellow and white peaches and nectarines, old classifications and new, favorites and moneymakers. "We used to own the land across the road," she said as we talked about how many acres there are. But some of the family members sold their parcels. This area has started to become Amador County's wine country overflow, and that means there's big money in the real estate—much more than farming can make.

And when I sit in my kitchen and peel the ripe nectarines and peaches in silence, stripping away the protective outer skin, which has been bred thinner and thinner so we can easily steal the luscious sunset-colored interior at our own discretion, I think of something that Camelia said: "Every generation could be the one that gives this all up." It makes me unbearably devastated. Much like how I feel about the orchard, which produces a necessary and tangible product—edible art—for the world to consume. And it's not valued or protected as it should be.

1 (17.3-ounce) box frozen puff pastry sheets (preferably Pepperidge Farm), thawed overnight in the fridge

4½ to 5 pounds ripe yellow peaches or yellow nectarines

½ to 1 cup granulated sugar (see Note)

1 teaspoon cornstarch

1 pinch kosher salt

1 egg

1 teaspoon water

Confectioners' sugar for dusting

Preheat the oven to 400°F. Line a baking sheet with parchment paper. Flour a work surface.

Place each puff pastry sheet on the prepared surface and cut each sheet into nine squares. With a rolling pin, give the squares a little roll to stretch out the dough, making them slightly larger squares.

Peel, pit, and thinly slice the peaches until you have 5 cups of fruit. In a bowl, toss the peach slices with ½ cup of the granulated sugar, the cornstarch, and salt. Taste the peaches and add more sugar if needed. Place about 2 tablespoons of the peaches in the center of a puff pastry square, then place another puff pastry square on top, encasing the filling. Firmly press the edges to slightly seal; you want some of the filling to spill out.

continued ▶

In a small bowl, whisk the egg and water to create an egg wash. With a pastry brush, brush the squares with the egg wash and place on the prepared baking sheet.

Bake for 12 to 15 minutes, or until the pastry is browned. Transfer to a wire rack and let cool for 5 minutes.

Dust the pastelillos with confectioners' sugar and serve warm.

Note: The amount of sugar you add to the peaches or nectarines will vary greatly, depending on where and when you're getting the fruit. If they're in season and you're getting them directly from the orchard or farmers' market, you'll probably need less sugar. But, if your only option is to get them from the supermarket, you'll probably need more sugar.

June Pride yellow peach, Twin Peaks Orchard, Placer County, California.

Camelia Enriquez Miller packs peaches, Twin Peaks Orchard.

Picking the crop, Twin Peaks Orchard.

Ready for market.

TWIN PEAKS

PRODUCE OF U.S.A.

TWIN PEAKS
Organic Red Haven Yellow Peach
Count 124.21

PRODUCE OF U.S.A.

TWIN PEAKS
White Lady White Peach
Count 180.21

Quesitos de Queso y Guayaba

Makes about 18 quesitos

Quesitos and pastelillos (the dessert kind, not the savory kind) are exemplary examples of European pastry making and one of the few good things that colonization brought to the island. These little pastries are meant for rich people, which is probably why my grandma never made them. Quesitos and pastelillos use the same puff pastry dough; the only difference between the two is the shape and the filling. Traditionally, quesitos contained only cheese; but as time went on, we required more and more from the little pastry. What most people don't know is that it's traditional to brush the tops of the finished pastry with a simple syrup (some people add honey to the syrup), giving it an inviting shine. I go one extra step, for the sake of being extra, and sprinkle sanding sugar on top while the simple syrup is still warm. The big granules of sanding sugar give the pastry a nice crunch.

1 (17.3-ounce) box frozen puff pastry sheets (preferably Pepperidge Farm), thawed overnight in the fridge

1 pound cream cheese

1 (14-ounce) block guava paste

¼ cup granulated sugar

1 tablespoon water

Sanding sugar for sprinkling (optional)

Preheat the oven to 400°F. Line a baking sheet with parchment paper. Flour a work surface.

Place each puff pastry sheet on the prepared surface and cut each sheet into nine squares. With a rolling pin, give the squares a little roll to stretch out the dough, making them slightly larger squares (you'll need more surface area for the guava paste).

Cut a ¼-inch-thick slice from the cream cheese and lay it diagonally in the center of a pastry square. Cut a ¼-inch-thick slice of guava paste and lay it directly on top of the cream cheese. Fold one side of the pastry over the filling and then bring the opposite side over the first; the filling should now be swaddled and peeking out from both ends. Repeat with the remaining puff pastry, cream cheese, and guava paste.

Bake for 10 to 15 minutes, or until the pastry is golden brown, keeping a close watch on them so they don't scorch.

While the quesitos are in the oven, in a small saucepan over medium heat, combine the granulated sugar and water, warming the mixture just enough to melt the sugar and make a simple syrup.

When the pastry is golden brown, take the pan out of the oven, immediately brush the quesitos with the simple syrup and sprinkle with sanding sugar, if desired. Place on a wire rack and let cool for 5 minutes before serving. (You don't want a mouth of molten guava paste.)

Apple Empanadillas

Makes 6 empanadillas

I always coarsely chop my apples, leaving some in large chunks and others super-fine because I like the final mixture to have various textures—gloppy, chunky, and crisp.

Apple Filling

8 Golden Delicious apples

1 splash apple cider vinegar

½ cup packed light brown sugar

2 tablespoons European-style butter

1 tablespoon pumpkin pie spice

1 pinch kosher salt

3 tablespoons cornstarch

1 teaspoon water

Empanadilla Dough

2½ cups all-purpose flour

1 pinch kosher salt

½ cup vegetable shortening or manteca

½ cup water with a few ice cubes

2 cups granulated sugar

2 tablespoons pumpkin pie spice

Canola oil for frying

To make the filling: Peel, core, and coarsely chop the apples. Place in a large bowl and toss with the vinegar.

In a large pot over medium heat, combine the apples, brown sugar, butter, pumpkin pie spice, and salt and stir to mix. Turn the heat to low and let simmer for 10 to 15 minutes to cook down the apples. Stir every now and then, ensuring that the mixture doesn't stick to the bottom of the pot. Once the apples have reached the texture you like, in a tiny bowl, stir together the cornstarch and water to make a slurry. Stir the slurry into the apples, turn off the heat, and let cool for 30 minutes.

To make the dough: In a large bowl, combine the flour and salt. Add the shortening and cut it into the flour with a fork or your hands until the mixture becomes the size of peas. Remove the ice from the water and add the water to the flour mixture and stir with the fork to incorporate.

Lightly flour a work surface. Gather the dough and separate into six equal pieces on the prepared surface. Using a rolling pin, roll each piece into a 3¼-inch circle. Using a 3-inch biscuit cutter, cut out a circle from each disc, discarding the scraps. Place 1 tablespoon of the filling on one half of a disc. Fold over the other half of the dough and use the fork tines to seal the empanadilla. Repeat to form the remaining discs.

Line a plate with paper towels. In a shallow bowl, stir together the granulated sugar and pumpkin pie spice. Set both near the stove. Fill a 10-inch cast-iron skillet with 2 inches of canola oil and place over medium-low heat. You want enough oil to partially cover the empanadillas. Heat the oil until it registers 350°F on an instant-read thermometer. (Sprinkle in a little flour; if the oil sizzles, it's ready for frying.)

Add three of the empanadillas to the oil and fry for 3 to 5 minutes on each side, or until brown, using tongs to flip them. Transfer the empanadillas to the bowl of spiced sugar, turning them to coat, and then place them on the prepared plate. Repeat to cook the remaining empanadillas.

Serve the empanadillas immediately.

Note: The yield varies with the size of dough rounds you roll. I use a 3-inch biscuit cutter, but you could make larger or smaller ones.

Cazuela

Makes 8 to 12 servings

Pre-cut and pre-portioned pumpkin and sweet potato are commonly found in some markets. I definitely take advantage of this. While I have seen cazuela made from scratch and cooked over a live fire, sometimes my schedule and kitchen don't allow for this romantic style of cooking. The size of the dice isn't entirely important; just know that the more uniform the pieces of pumpkin and sweet potato are, the more evenly they'll cook.

1-pound pumpkin, peeled and diced

1-pound sweet potato, peeled and diced

1 cup coconut milk

2 eggs, beaten

2 tablespoons light brown sugar

1 teaspoon pumpkin pie spice

1 teaspoon vanilla extract

1 pinch salt

1 cup all-purpose flour

Preheat the oven to 350°F. Line a 9 by 13-inch cake pan with a banana leaf, parchment paper, or aluminum foil.

Fill a pot with water and place over medium-high heat. Bring to a boil, add the pumpkin and sweet potato, and let boil for 10 to 15 minutes, or until they are super-fork-tender. Drain the pumpkin and sweet potato and transfer to a large bowl. Using a potato masher, mash the pumpkin and sweet potato until they are the consistency of mashed potatoes. While the mixture is still hot, pass through a fine-mesh sieve or tamis over another bowl. This will make the mixture super-smooth.

Add the coconut milk, eggs, brown sugar, pumpkin pie spice, vanilla, and salt to the mash and, using a rubber spatula, combine well. Add the flour and mix thoroughly. Pour the batter into the prepared cake pan and tap the pan against a flat surface to remove any air pockets.

Place the cake pan in a larger baking pan. Add hot tap water to the larger baking pan until it reaches three-fourths of the way up the outside of the inner pan, creating a water bath. Bake for 45 minutes to 1 hour, or until the cake is firm and creamy.

Serve the cazuela hot from the oven, at room temperature, or cold.

Flan de Queso

Makes 6 to 8 servings

I don't like flan—cue dry heaves. Most flans tend to be wiggly, in a bad way, and slippery in texture. Yet leave it to Puerto Ricans to take a traditional Spanish recipe and turn it up to 11. When people hear *cheese*, I know they don't think of Puerto Rico. But, Puerto Ricans love cheese! Some of us have it every morning with our breakfasts. Adding the cream cheese to this recipe gives the flan more of a smooth and rich cheesecake texture that *always* seems to impress and shock those who are trying it for the first time and making it hard for anyone to pass up.

12 ounces cream cheese, at room temperature

1 (14-ounce) can sweetened condensed milk

1 (12-ounce) can evaporated milk

4 eggs

1 teaspoon vanilla extract

1 pinch kosher salt

1½ cups granulated sugar

Preheat the oven to 350°F.

In a blender or food processor, combine the cream cheese, condensed milk, evaporated milk, eggs, vanilla, and salt and blend to form a thoroughly smooth batter.

Add the sugar to a small, wide pot and place over medium-high heat. Once the sugar starts to melt, turn the heat to medium and cook for 5 to 10 minutes, watching the sugar turn amber brown but no darker. Make sure you keep an eye on it; the sugar quickly turns from caramelized to burnt. Pour the caramelized sugar into an 8-inch square baking dish, tilting the dish to evenly distribute the caramel. Work quickly because the caramel will start to harden as soon as you pour it into the baking dish.

Place the baking dish in a larger baking pan, then pour the batter directly over the caramel. Add hot tap water to the larger baking pan until it reaches three-fourths of the way up the outside of the inner dish, creating a water bath. Cover the larger baking pan with aluminum foil. Bake for 1 hour, or until a toothpick inserted in the center of the flan comes out clean.

Remove the baking dish from the water bath and set on a wire rack to completely cool. Once cool, run a knife around the edges of the flan. Place a serving plate over the top of the baking dish (make sure the plate is big enough to entirely cover the edges of the dish) and invert to unmold the flan. Gently lift away the baking dish, and hopefully the flan will release from it onto the serving plate.

Serve the flan immediately.

Note: You know those people who say not to touch the sugar when you're making caramel? We don't know them. All the Puerto Rican women that I've seen make the caramel for this dish liberally move the sugar around as it cooks.

Budin with Walnuts

Makes 8 to 12 servings

Like many Spanish words that have evolved into a particular Puerto Rican Spanish, *pudin*—which translates to "pudding," an umbrella term for desserts—somehow changed to *budin* over the course of the years. The earliest known Puerto Rican cookbook was written in 1859 and has a recipe for this bread pudding creation, titled Pudin de Leche. The 1859 recipe contains bread with the crusts removed, milk, butter, cinnamon, cloves, raisins, toasted almonds, and lemon zest; is cooked over an open fire; and is topped with candied almonds. Needless to say, Puerto Ricans' love of bread pudding runs as deep as their need to make something out of nothing.

There are very few bread puddings that I have yet to love, mostly because I'm a texture person. I don't love mush. I need crunch. Luckily, California happens to be the world's top producer of almonds and walnuts. I don't need to go far to reach a walnut orchard (or a neighborhood tree) where I can simply pluck the plump shells from their branches and crack them open to reveal their gnarled velvetiness. Walnuts have a dark and robust flavor that are perfect for sweet shit.

.

¾ cup salted butter

1 cup packed light brown sugar

1 (1½-pound) loaf day-old bread

3 cups coconut milk

1 (14-ounce) can sweetened condensed milk

3 eggs

2 tablespoons pumpkin pie spice

1 tablespoon vanilla extract

1 pinch kosher salt

1½ cups chopped walnuts

Preheat the oven to 350°F. Line a 9 by 13-inch baking pan with parchment paper.

Put ½ cup of the butter and the brown sugar in the prepared pan, spread into an even layer, and put in the oven for 5 to 10 minutes, or until the sugar starts to melt and slowly caramelize.

Meanwhile, cut the bread into irregular pieces, place in a large bowl, and set aside.

In a small saucepan over low heat, melt the remaining ¼ cup butter. In another large bowl, combine the coconut milk, condensed milk, eggs, pumpkin pie spice, vanilla, salt, and melted butter and mix well. Pour the mixture over the bread and set aside for about 15 minutes, or until absorbed completely.

Remove the baking pan from the oven and swirl it around to ensure the butter and sugar are incorporated. Sprinkle the walnuts into the pan, then pour the bread mush over the nuts and sugar-butter mixture.

Bake for 40 minutes to 1 hour, or until a toothpick inserted in the center comes out clean. Place a serving tray over the pan and invert to release the budin onto the tray.

Serve the budin warm.

Arroz con Dulce

Makes 8 to 12 servings

Every Christmas, there it was. The pot of white blob, strewn with black polka dots, that no one but Nana and Mami seemed to enjoy. I would later come to know this as rice pudding, or arroz con dulce. This dish is traditionally eaten cold, so if you can wait the four hours it takes to cool completely before being consumed, this one is for you. But if you want to eat it hot or warm, who am I to stop you?

2½ cups water

2 cinnamon sticks, plus ground cinnamon for sprinkling

1 knob peeled ginger, sliced in half

1 (15-ounce) can coconut milk

½ (12-ounce) can evaporated milk

1 cup medium-grain rice, washed (see page 11)

1 tablespoon salted butter

1 pinch kosher salt

1 vanilla bean, or 1 teaspoon vanilla extract

½ (13.5-ounce) can cream of coconut

¾ cup granulated sugar

½ cup packed light brown sugar

¼ cup raisins (optional)

1½ teaspoons pumpkin pie spice

In a traditional caldero or a wide, shallow stainless-steel pot over medium-high heat, combine the water, cinnamon sticks, and ginger. Bring to a rolling boil, about 10 minutes, and then remove and discard the ginger. Turn the heat to medium.

Add the coconut milk, evaporated milk, rice, butter, and salt to the cinnamon water. Split the vanilla bean pod and scrape the seeds into the rice mixture; add the pod as well. Stir in the cream of coconut, granulated sugar, brown sugar, raisins (if using), and pumpkin pie spice. Let simmer slowly, covered, for 15 to 20 minutes, or until it is the consistency of oatmeal. Remove the vanilla pod, if used.

Spoon the pudding into serving dishes, or leave it in the caldero if you prefer to serve it family-style. Sprinkle with ground cinnamon and refrigerate, uncovered, until completely cool, at least 4 hours or up to overnight.

Serve the pudding cold.

The Evolution of Mallorcas

Fluffy and pleasantly sweet, mallorcas travel well across breakfast cultures. Originally called *ensaïmadas* in Catalan, they were first documented in the late eighteenth century—although they likely had been made for centuries before that—when a Franciscan friar began collecting and recording a number of recipes from the Balearic Islands, the eastern Spanish archipelago that includes Mallorca. As he noted, bakers there would roll out the yeasty enriched dough, spread it with lard (called *saïm* in Catalan, from which the bread's original name derives), shape it into its signature coil, and bake it until risen and golden.

According to Tomeu Arbona, owner of El Fornet de la Soca bakery in Palma, Mallorca, the bread's first bakers were likely Sephardic Jews, and ensaïmadas were originally a sweet bread baked for the Sabbath, similar to challah. While the earliest versions were likely made using kosher butter or oil, there are records of Jews switching to baking with lard—decidedly against their beliefs—during the massacres and persecution led by the Catholic Church in the fourteenth and fifteenth centuries. While many Jews continued to practice their faith in secret during that time, some of them cooked with lard to convince the Church of their loyalty.

Centuries later, mallorcas are a staple at bakeries in San Juan, thanks to Antonio Rigo, who, in 1900, crossed the Atlantic from Felanitx, Mallorca, with his family recipe in tow. Within two years, he'd opened Mallorquina Bakery, which ultimately became La Bombonera, a café that still makes some of the best mallorcas on the island. The bread swiftly took on a life of its own there, ultimately manifesting as the sweet, griddled ham-and-cheese versions found today in cafés across San Juan.

The legacy of mallorcas, though, is still on the move. In New Orleans, self-taught Puerto Rican baker Diego Martin Pérez is making his own version—the one that I brought home—with wild yeasts and freshly milled heirloom grains. Unlike the mallorcas that I've had in San Juan, Martin Pérez's are hefty but have a strong rise and distinct sourdough aroma. He says that while he was growing up in Puerto Rico, the baked treat represented "sheer nostalgia." There was a bakery across the street from Martin Pérez's school, and mallorcas were his after-school snack. If he went alone, he'd get a plain, single mallorca, toasted. If he went with his mom, they'd get six at a time. In New Orleans, Martin Pérez has found a new market for his hometown pastries— bridging yet another great distance.

Mallorcas

Makes 8 to 12 mallorcas

When I preheat my cast-iron comal and slip a pat of butter onto the surface, I can't help but remember a moment when I'd just gotten home from New Orleans. At an artisanal bakery there, I'd purchased a mallorca, a sweet spiral bun made by a baker from Puerto Rico, who was following a centuries-old formula that can be traced back to a tiny island off the coast of Spain. After I removed the pastry from my backpack, where I'd kept it safe and unsquashed on the two thousand-plus-mile journey, I sliced it in half and set the halves cut-side down on the griddle. I then made a sandwich like the ones often found in Puerto Rico, with some crispy bacon and melted American cheese, a decadent treat made even more so by the traditional snowfall of confectioners' sugar that I dusted over the top. At home in California, every time that I repeat this ritual, I recognize that the mallorcas' journey isn't over yet.

10 tablespoons unsalted butter, at room temperature

1 cup warm (about 120°F) water

1 teaspoon dry yeast

1 teaspoon granulated sugar, plus ½ cup

1 cup warm (about 120°F) milk

1 teaspoon vanilla extract

3 eggs, beaten

6 cups all-purpose flour

1 teaspoon kosher salt

1 cup confectioners' sugar

Preheat the oven to 350°F.

In a small pot over low heat, melt 4 tablespoons of the butter. Set aside.

In a small bowl, combine the water, yeast, and 1 teaspoon granulated sugar. Give it a little mix and set aside for 5 minutes, or until the top of the liquid looks foamy. In another small bowl, combine the milk, melted butter, vanilla, and eggs and stir to incorporate.

In a stand mixer fitted with the paddle attachment (or in a large bowl with a wooden spoon), thoroughly combine the flour, salt, and remaining ½ cup granulated sugar. Add the yeast-water and one-third of the egg mixture and mix on medium speed for 10 minutes, or until the dough starts to make a slapping sound. Add the remaining egg mixture, a bit at a time, and blend together; you want to make sure the flour is absorbing all the liquid before adding more, but you also don't want to add too much liquid. Once the dough starts to tighten and it becomes too much work for the mixer (or you), grab a plastic bench scraper and start to knead the dough. You need to mix only until all the flour is fully incorporated; the dough will be tacky. Cover with plastic wrap and let rest in a warm place for 1 to 2 hours.

Smear the bottom of a baking sheet with 1 tablespoon butter, oil a large bowl, and flour a work surface.

continued ▶

Scrape the dough onto the prepared surface. With the bench scraper, knead and fold the dough for 5 to 7 minutes, or until it's no longer tacky. It will be pretty moist and absorb the flour on the bench scraper. If you need more flour, it's fine to add a handful at a time. Continue to work the dough until it's soft and supple. Place the dough in the prepared bowl and turn it to lightly coat. Cover the bowl with plastic wrap and let rest in a warm place for 30 minutes.

Clean your work surface and then re-flour. Place the dough onto the prepared surface. Flour a rolling pin and roll out the dough into an amorphous rectangle, about ¼ inch thick. With the bench scraper, cut a 1-inch strip off the edge of the dough. With both hands, roll the strip against the work surface to create a cylindrical rope. Arrange that rope into a snail-like coil, tucking the end under the coil. Scoop up the coiled mallorca with the scraper and place on the prepared baking sheet. Repeat with the rest of the dough.

In a small pot over low heat, melt the remaining 5 tablespoons butter. With a pastry brush, brush 2 tablespoons butter over the mallorcas. Cover the baking sheet with plastic wrap and let rest in a warm place for 30 minutes.

Bake for 15 to 30 minutes, or until the mallorcas are firm and *sliiiightly* brown. Place the baking sheet on a wire rack, brush the mallorcas with the remaining 3 tablespoons melted butter, and let cool completely.

Dust the mallorcas with the confectioners' sugar all over—douse 'em!—before serving.

Note: Mallorcas can be frozen; after you shape the dough into the snail-like coils, instead of baking, just put them in freezer storage containers and they'll keep for up to 6 months. Bake from frozen on a baking sheet in a 350°F oven for 20 to 30 minutes. You can also use mallorcas to take the place of buns for hamburgers and in bread in the iconic ham-and-cheese breakfast sandwich.

Tembleque

Makes 4 servings

Yes, you could totally make this with fresh coconuts—the brown ones with the hairs, not the young green coconuts—but just because you can access coconuts doesn't mean you want to take on the task of puncturing the hard exterior with a hammer to extract the coconut water. I'm just going to take the easy route. And I can hear the groans of a thousand Diasporicans.

2 (13.5-ounce) cans full-fat unsweetened coconut milk

¾ cup granulated sugar

1 pinch kosher salt

1 cinnamon stick

½ cup cornstarch

⅓ cup unsweetened coconut flakes

Confectioners' sugar for sprinkling

Pumpkin pie spice for garnishing

Add the coconut milk, granulated sugar, salt, and cinnamon stick to a medium pot and place over low heat. Let simmer for 1 to 2 minutes to steep the mixture, then discard the cinnamon stick. Whisk in the cornstarch and continuously whisk until the mixture is free of lumps, continuing to simmer for 10 to 15 minutes, or until the mixture reaches a custardy consistency. Remove from the heat and let cool for about 30 minutes, or until it reaches room temperature.

Rinse four 4-inch ramekins with water. Pour the custard mixture into the ramekins, tap against a flat surface to remove any air pockets, and then place the ramekins on a baking sheet. Cover with plastic wrap and refrigerate for at least 4 hours or up to overnight.

Preheat the oven to 350°F.

Spread the coconut flakes on a baking sheet. Roast the flakes, tossing every few minutes, for 5 to 10 minutes, or until the coconut begins to brown. Transfer the flakes to a mixing bowl and sprinkle with confectioners' sugar.

Run a knife along the inside edge of each ramekin. Quickly invert one ramekin onto a serving plate, tap the bottom, and gently lift away to (hopefully) release the tembleque. Repeat with the other ramekins.

Garnish the tembleques with pumpkin pie spice and the coconut flakes and serve.

Coquito

Makes 6 to 8 servings

As with much of history in cultures that pass down traditions orally, it's hard to track the origins of coquito, Puerto Rico's rum punch that's served during the holidays. The most common story goes that the first coquito was created with pitorro, a moonshine rum made from sugarcane and then buried underground to ferment. You would combine that with fresh coconut water and, later, grated coconut. You might also customize your pitorro with tropical fruits. (My grandmother used tamarind.) The bad news is that unless you know someone, you're not likely to ever taste pitorro in Puerto Rico as it's illegal even though tolerated. The good news is that a company called Port Morris Distillery in the Bronx makes pitorro for sale. Today, the silky libation (pictured opposite, lower right) is embedded in the holiday repertoire of Puerto Rican families. Warming spices such as cinnamon, ginger, and cloves are commonly included. Some use eggs when making coquito, while others would never do so.

If you want to go old-school with your coquito, you might stick a piece of cheese, typically Edam, or what locals call queso de bola, in the finished bottle. The rum infuses the cheese, which you can remove and serve with crackers when it's time to drink your coquito.

2 cups coconut milk

1 (15-ounce) can cream of coconut

1 (14-ounce) can condensed milk

2 cups gold rum (preferably Ron del Barrilito Two Star)

2 teaspoons ground cinnamon

$\frac{1}{2}$ teaspoon ground ginger

$\frac{1}{2}$ teaspoon ground nutmeg

$\frac{1}{2}$ teaspoon ground cardamom

$\frac{1}{4}$ teaspoon ground cloves

1 pinch kosher salt

Ice cubes for serving

In a blender, combine the coconut milk, cream of coconut, condensed milk, rum, cinnamon, ginger, nutmeg, cardamom, cloves, and salt and blend on high speed until well combined. Transfer to a 2-quart bottle or canning jar with an airtight lid and refrigerate for up to 4 months.

Shake well before serving over ice.

Maví and Hibiscus Cooler

Makes 6 to 8 servings

Maví is an ancient drink fossilized in the minds and stories of our ancestors. You'd be hard-pressed to find this hoppy-tasting beverage (pictured on page 229, middle right) outside of the island. (In the Barbados and Trinidad, it is known as mauby.) Maví is made by simmering the bark from the snakewood tree and can commonly be found at roadside stands throughout Puerto Rico, sometimes mixed with aromatics and botanicals. When allowed to sit and ferment, maví can become slightly alcoholic. It is an acquired taste, so I combined it with one of my favorite summertime drinks, agua de jamaica. Add the rum if you like, but it still makes a stellar drink without the alcohol.

8 cups tap water

3 cups dried hibiscus flowers (see Note)

2 ounces maví bark (see Note)

1 cup granulated sugar, or as needed

Ice cubes for serving

6 to 8 cups sparkling mineral water

White rum for serving (optional)

Pour the tap water into a pot, place over high heat, and bring to a boil. Stir in the hibiscus, maví, and sugar to taste and turn the heat to low. Let simmer for 12 to 15 minutes, then turn off the heat, set aside, and allow to cool completely, about 1 hour. Strain the liquid and discard the hibiscus and maví. Transfer to a 2-quart bottle or canning jar with an airtight lid and refrigerate for up to 1 week.

When ready to serve, fill a pint glass with ice, add 1 cup of the mixture and 1 cup of the sparkling mineral water, stir to combine, and top with a splash of rum, if desired.

Notes: You can find hibiscus flowers at local Mexican markets.

If you live outside Puerto Rico, the only way to access maví is online.

Roasted Piña Colada

Makes 6 servings

The battle of who invented the piña colada (created in the 1960s) persists in Puerto Rico. Was it created at the Caribe Hilton? Not according to the plaque outside Barrachina restaurant in Viejo San Juan. Burn, Caribe Hilton! The piña coladas that you'll commonly find on the island are quickly made with canned pineapple juice, Coco Lopez, and rum; quickly blitzed in the blender (or a continuously rotating slushy machine); and quickly served without irony (and without joy) to the hordes of tourists who insist on perpetuating the idea that Puerto Rico is a paradise to which the wealthy and clueless quickly escape. Quick, quick, quick. *Thee* end. The roasted pineapple in this recipe gives the drink a two-dimensional flavor profile and slows down the process. You want this drink (pictured on page 229, upper left)? You're gonna have to work for it.

1 medium pineapple, peeled and cut into chunks

1 tablespoon granulated sugar

1 (15-ounce) can cream of coconut (preferably Coco Lopez)

White rum, to taste

Gold rum (preferably Ron del Barrilito Two Star), to taste

6 cups ice cubes

Water as needed

Preheat the oven to 350°F.

Place the pineapple in a roasting pan, sprinkle with the sugar, and roast for 10 to 20 minutes, or just until it has softened and turned golden brown. Remove from the pan and let completely cool.

In a blender, combine the roasted pineapple, cream of coconut, both rums, and the ice and blitz until the mixture is thick and smooth but still fluid. If it's too stiff, add some water to loosen it, eyeballing the amount.

Serve the piña coladas immediately.

Jesus, Rancho Llano Seco, Butte County, California.

Chef Christian Godbold, San Francisco, California.

Hans Haverman and Heidi Rhodes,
H&H Fresh Fish Co., Santa Cruz, California.

Lyman Chan,
San Francisco,
California.

Acknowledgments

It's often said that writing and being a writer is a solitary affair. It used to be. We all know that in this day and age, cookbook writing takes the backseat to all other jobs as you have to be your own damn marketing person, agent, administrator, researcher, social media curator, housekeeper, cook . . . the list goes on. When you're a Brown or Black person, a community is not only helpful, it's necessary. When "101 ways to Instant-Pot black beans on Keto while also doing Paleo" has been done for the umpteenth time, you need someone who's going to understand why your book isn't getting published without you having to explain why your book isn't getting published: whiteness. Because when you're a Brown or Black person, you can know everyone in the damn industry, have a mentorship with José Andrés, publish numerous articles in print and on the Web, have a column with the *San Francisco Chronicle*, be the first Puerto Rican food columnist in the country, win an IACP award for best narrative writing, have the support of Rancho Gordo founder Steve Sando, and get introduced to one of the only Puerto Rican editors turned agents in the business, and still . . . no one will publish your book. By the way, the person that I just described is me, in case you didn't know. When you've done everything that other authors have told you to do that worked for them, and it doesn't work, the only difference that you can see is . . . the whiteness you lack. To think that the color of your skin is the one thing standing in your way is really fucked up to carry through life.

Because of this, these thank-yous are so much more than thank-yous. These thank-yous are lifelines. These thank-yous are the very sole reason that I have gotten to this point. To these thank-yous, I owe so much.

To my cuñado, Dan Liberti, thank you for taking photos of my stuff for the last decade. Although we might not always see eye to eye, I still admire your craft and appreciate you. You have taught me so much about the business side of being a freelance artist. I'm not sure that I ever thought about creating a cookbook before you said, "We should do a cookbook," in 2014. It was a gift. And a curse. And you're also related to one of my favorite people . . . Mila. You made this childless only child an aunty/tia/titi. And thanks to the other key players on our photography team, food and prop stylist Jillian Knox and assistant food stylist Malina Syvoravong, for all their behind-the-scenes work to make the recipes look great for the camera.

To Lorena Jones, thank you for never saying die. Thank you for offering me a solid deal even when I didn't and don't have an agent. When everyone else said my book was too "memoir-y," which was apparently unusual for cookbooks, you saw it as storytelling. You never told me to ditch the memories, the stories, or the grandma. Thank you for your patience, understanding, and vision.

To the ones who tried: Thank you, José Andrés, for using every contact you had to help me make my dream come true. Thank you for actually "being about it" and giving me a once-in-a-lifetime job opportunity in New York City to cook for Steven Spielberg and Rita Moreno. Thank you for follow-up phone calls and emails. Thank you for just supporting me in a time when I felt like no one was listening. I will always be indebted to you, con cariño. Thank you, Julia Turshen, for trying not once or twice but multiple times to reset the button and put me on the right path. I always felt bad that you tried so hard and nothing came of it. And Steve Sando, thank you for scraping me off the floor and giving me a purpose during my time in exile.

To my best friend since elementary school, my Day One, my baby blue blad, Yolanda Jackson. Thank you for keeping me grounded.

To the advisors: Shawn Walker-Smith and Tina Ramos, thank you for keeping me honest. You have been more than just good friends. You've been recipe testers, traveling companions, truth-tellers, transportation, moral support, dining companions, and translators. You've pointed out so many of my flaws but allowed me to grow from my unknowing mistakes and never ghosted me. Thanks to Alicia Kennedy for literally being the reason that I even have a fucking newsletter and a source of income. I'm in awe of your ability to write at the confluence of food and politics.

To the mentors: Thank you, Papa Paolo Lucchesi, for seeing something in me that I didn't even see in myself. You are one of the most patient and nurturing editors of which anyone could ever dream. You made me the first Puerto Rican food columnist in the country. Thank you, Carole Ching and Mary Garza, for believing in me since I was sixteen years old. You took the place of a maternal figure when I had little to no contact with my own mother. Thanks to Teresa Urkofsky and James Chavez, my memorable culinary school instructors, who I'm lucky enough to now call friends.

To the Puerto Ricans: Thank you, Eric Rivera, Jessica Von Dop DeJesus, Cesar Ramos, Jeremie Serrano, Reina Gascon-Lopez, Cristina Baez, Rafael Ruiz, Erika P. Rodriguez, Roberto Perez, Caribe Casual Shop, Santurce Vintage, Joseph Cuevas, Paxx Caraballo Moll, Pedro Alvarez, Alcor Foods, and Peter Chenaux.

To the one I failed: Thanks, Dylan S., for introducing me to music. I'm so sorry for everything.

To cousin Ivan Diaz, thanks for being everything—doorman, Mami's aide, mule, chauffeur, equalizer, male handshaker, translator, chauvinistic business associate, proxy, swimming companion, and comedic relief. I'm sorry we don't always see eye to eye.

To those who were resources for me: Christina Edmondson, David Santana, Damien Cabrera, Rodney Blackwell, Celeste Noche, Tunde Wey, Eric Kim, Alex Lau, the Khamsalys, Alex Tenette, Gustavo Arellano, Alisson Xavier, and Norma Quon and Lyman Chan.

To the Medicis: Terri Carter, Danette Negron, Frida Pilar, Diana Dich, Josmine Evans, Patrick Thomas, Vanessa Nunez, Nathalie Christian, Mellisa Nelson, Julian Wade, Danielle Giddens, Alisha Miranda, Jennifer Jerutis, Erica Stinemates, Chantal Hazlett, Nicole Tourtelot, Lisa Prodanovich, Billie-Jean Martin, Kat Campbell, Sara Floor, Quyen Chavez, Enrique Grijalva, Daphne K. Jenkins, Megan Walsh, Vivian Ho, Laura Gamble, Carolyn Reed, Kat Campbell, and Marissa and Charlie Thieriot.

To the Ten Speed team: Thanks to Betsy Stromberg, for being our creative director and designer and for pointing out when I was being . . . impatient. Many thanks, too, to production editors Doug Ogan and Sohayla Farman, production manager Serena Sigona, publicist Felix Cruz, and marketer Brianne Sperber.

Thanks to H&H Fresh Fish for giving a shit about producing, sourcing, and offering some of the most amazing seafood. To Hog Island Oyster Co., thanks for allowing us to traipse around the property so I could brag about your oysters to the world. And to Rancho Llano Seco: I'm speechless in awe.

And to everyone who contributed to getting me to the James Beard House in 2018. To everyone who contributed to getting me to Puerto Rico for the pilón and doughnuts research. And to everyone who contributed to the Puerto Ricans–in–Hawai'i research.

Index

Published in the United States by Ten Speed Press, an imprint of Random House,
a division of Penguin Random House LLC, New York.
TenSpeed.com
RandomHouseBooks.com

Ten Speed Press and the Ten Speed Press colophon are registered trademarks
of Penguin Random House LLC.

Grateful acknowledgment is made to Arte Público Press-University of Houston for
permission to reprint "Criollo Story" from *AmeRícan* by Tato Laviera, copyright © 2003
Arte Público Press-University of Houston. Reprinted with permission of the publisher.

Typefaces: Fontsmith's FS Kim and Monotype's Macklin Sans

Library of Congress Cataloging-in-Publication Data
  Names: Maisonet, Illyanna, author. | Twitty, Michael, 1977- writer of foreword.
  Title: Diasporican: a Puerto Rican cookbook / Illyanna Maisonet; foreword
    by Michael W. Twitty; Puerto Rico photographs by Erika P. Rodriguez;
    California and food photographs by Dan Liberti.
  Description: First edition. | New York: Ten Speed Press, [2022] |
    Includes index.
  Identifiers: LCCN 2021060872 (print) | LCCN 2021060873 (ebook) |
    ISBN 9781984859761 (hardcover) | ISBN 9781984859778 (ebook)
  Subjects: LCSH: Cooking, Puerto Rican. | LCGFT: Cookbooks.
  Classification: LCC TX716.P8 M35 2022 (print) | LCC TX716.P8 (ebook) |
    DDC 641.597295—dc23/eng/20211231
  LC record available at https://lccn.loc.gov/2021060872
  LC ebook record available at https://lccn.loc.gov/2021060873

Hardcover ISBN: 978-1-9848-5976-1
eBook ISBN: 978-1-9848-5977-8

Printed in China

Editor: Lorena Jones | Production editors: Doug Ogan and Sohayla Farman
Designer: Betsy Stromberg | Production designers: Mari Gill and Faith Hague
Production manager: Serena Sigona | Prepress color manager: Jane Chinn
Food and prop stylist: Jillian Knox | Food stylist assistant: Malina Syvoravong
Copyeditor: Mi Ae Lipe | Proofreader: Hope Clarke | Indexer: Amy Hall
Publicist: Felix Cruz | Marketer: Brianne Sperber

10 9 8 7 6 5 4 3 2 1

First Edition